MORE SERMONS IN STORIES

MORE SERMONS IN STORIES

By

WILLIAM L. STIDGER

ABINGDON-COKESBURY PRESS
New York • *Nashville*

MORE SERMONS IN STORIES

TO CLAY DOSS

"AND ALWAYS WHEN THE OLD YEAR ENDS
I CLASP MY ROSARY OF FRIENDS,
AND PAUSE TO BREATHE A GRATEFUL PRAYER
FOR EVERY BEAD OF FRIENDSHIP THERE."

CONTENTS

A WORD TO START THIS BOOK

"Tell me a story!" is the first and universal cry of a little child in its attempt to grow a soul and enlarge its horizons. Lynn Harold Hough in one of his early books, *The Little Old Lady,* tells of watching the little old lady read a story to a child. As he sits there musing, he tries to analyze the significance of this universal scene of a mother telling a story to a child, and he decides that this is the best way of keeping the soul of the world alive.

Jesus himself recognized that the short story, or parable, is the best form of preaching and the best way to keep the soul of the world alive. The parables of Jesus are good enough authority for any modern preacher if he really wants to get over a great and simple truth. Some writer has said that the first task of anybody who wants to move humanity is to take an abstract philosophical truth and put it into story form, and then he can move the world.

This book is sent forth with the hope that it may be useful to those who are dedicated to moving humanity—or some small part of it—to higher levels. Indications that *There Are Sermons in Stories* proved of some value, not only to ministers, speakers, and teachers, but also to parents and others who found the stories helpful in the daily period of personal or family worship, have made me bold to offer this new group of short, short stories.

WILLIAM L. STIDGER

"RUB WHAT OFF?"

YEARS ago when I was traveling in China, I picked up a parable about two balls which are typical of two types of people.

One of the balls was covered with a very thin layer of gold; the other was solid gold. They were put together in a box without any wrappings to protect them. The gilded ball was very careful of itself. It tried to keep very still because it knew that its slight covering would easily wear off—that the gold was not deep. But the ball that was gold all the way through did not care how much it rolled around in that box or bumped against its neighbor. It was sure of itself. It needed to take no precautions to protect itself, no matter how roughly it was treated.

The gilded ball, terrified lest its gilding be rubbed off by contact with the other ball, said to the solid gold one, "You had better be careful how you knock about or that stuff will wear off. You will rub it off by bumping about as you do, so carelessly."

"Rub what off?" asked the other ball.

Those who are true gold all through do not need to fear that they will rub anything off. Only those who have a cheap veneer of gold have that worry. Those who have real power of personality, real background, culture, and training, are sure of themselves. The others have to be continually protecting themselves, fighting for their prerogatives, making themselves a nuisance by always battling for what they call their rights. They are usually the carping, the critical, the gossiping types. The real ones have such a sense of power and assurance within themselves that they are not even aware of any necessity to criticize others. They do not run others down in order to protect their own weaknesses or to build up their own inner sense of certainty. "Rub what off?" is their almost naive query.

11

Abraham Lincoln loved to loaf in country stores and tell home-ly stories. He never felt it necessary to protect his dignity. He was gold all the way through and could afford to be honest, sincere, and simple. True greatness is always that way. Jesus loafed with fishermen and outcasts along the shores of Galilee. The truly great of the earth have never been afraid of rubbing off the external gilding, for they are gold all the way through.

When the world admonishes caution, they ask, "Rub what off?"

"NINETY-NINE AND A HALF WON'T DO!"

MY friend Dr. Ezra Cox, who works in home missions, spent several weeks recently among the Southern Negroes of the Methodist Church. He was accompanied by a famous Negro bishop on his rounds of preaching to the responsive Negroes.

One morning as the bishop was preaching a fervent sermon, an old mammy got up from her seat and started to dance up and down the aisle of the church. The bishop, evidently accustomed to such procedure, went on with his sermon as if nothing were happening.

After the sermon, Dr. Cox said to the woman, "Why did you get to dancing this morning when the bishop was preaching?"

Said the old mammy, "I tell you, frien', when I gets religion it makes de bottom o' my feet tickle and itch, and I jest gotta dance to 'spress myself. I jest gotta dance fo' de Lawd God Almighty!"

That evening the bishop took ill, Dr. Cox had to do the preaching. Just when he got well started he saw that same woman in his congregation, and he wondered if he would stir her into a dancing mood with his sermon as the bishop had done in the morning.

He preached his most fervent sermon and kept watching her, but she did no dancing that night. In fact, while she seemed to be listening intently, she did not move from her seat. He was discouraged, for he felt that his sermon must be a failure. He was talking about giving to missions, giving to help other people poorer than they were. But his words seemed to be falling on hard and stony ground as far as that woman was concerned. The preacher was disappointed.

Then suddenly toward the end of his sermon he noticed that old mammy begin to sway back and forth on her seat. Her eyes shone with fire. Sweet and low she began to sing an old Negro spiritual, which went in its chorus something like this:

> Lord, we gotta give one hundred per cent;
> Ninety-nine and a half won't do;
> Lord, we gotta give one hundred per cent,
> Ninety-nine and a half won't do.

She had hardly started when the whole church took up the refrain:

> Lord, we gotta give one hundred per cent;
> Ninety-nine and a half won't do.

He stopped his sermon to listen and then heard her improvise this phrase:

> I wanna tell Moses, I wanna tell Moses dat
> We gotta give one hundred per cent;
> Ninety-nine and a half won't do!

Each stanza started off with the names of some Biblical character, "I wanna tell Moses, . . . I wanna tell Isaiah, . . .I wanna tell Amos, . . . I wanna tell John, . . . I wanna tell Jesus dat . . . Ninety-nine and a half won't do!"

It was a stirring experience to hear that response to his challenge; and it was thrilling to me to see how it links up with our needs now. We can't get by with halfhearted giving of our money, our time, our labor, our loyalty.

> We gotta give one hundred per cent;
> Ninety-nine and a half won't do!

13

"PERHAPS YOU KNOW MY BOY?"

RECENTLY I spoke at a theological seminary in Hartford, Connecticut. After my talk a slender old man cordially invited me to have lunch at his home. I was in a hurry to get away and would much rather have gone on my journey and eaten at a restaurant; but he was such a kindly person I didn't want to offend him, and so I went over to his home. Being careless in catching names at introductions, I didn't know his name and was ashamed of myself. However, we had a pleasant visit; the lunch was served, and we had a jolly good time eating it.

Following the meal we sat and talked. He told me that he had been a missionary in China for thirty years but was now retired and working part time, teaching a course in missions in the seminary. I remember feeling sorry for him and all retired missionaries who are forced to return to America because of age or war. We talked of that for a time, and I expressed my sympathy for him. I even felt in my heart a sense of pity, because I thought I knew that he must be living on short rations, for missionaries are not able to save much money.

Finally he began to tell me a story about his son, who was born and reared in China. His story ran like this:

"My boy came back to the United States because he had a scheme for a new type of magazine which he thought he might be able to work out, in spite of the fact that the magazine field was already crowded and many of those who were already in it were failing and going to the wall.

"But my boy thought he had a new and unique idea of what he called a 'news weekly' which, if he could manage to finance it, might go over in a big way."

That gentle old man smiled in what looked to be an indulgent way. That smile deceived me, and I immediately assumed, without much reason, that his son had tried and failed in his enterprise. Then that lonely old missionary went on. And all the time he was talking I was searching my mind trying to remember his

14

name, which I had carelessly missed in our introduction. But the old man continued:

"I had saved six hundred dollars in my thirty years as a missionary in China; so when my boy Henry, stranded in Chicago, sent and asked me to lend him that six hundred dollars—the savings of a lifetime—I sent it at once, although I wasn't very sure that his enterprise would succeed. It was that six hundred dollars which kept him while he financed his new magazine.

"Now he is doing fairly well, is Henry."

I was still stretching my mind to remember the name, and that old man evidently saw my inner agitation for he said, "You know my boy Henry, don't you?"

I tried to mumble something which would not embarrass either of us, and then I noticed a letter on his worn desk. It was addressed to H. W. Luce, and in the upper left corner was the familiar name *Time*. A light broke over my mind, and I suddenly recognized that I was sitting in the humble home and in the kindly presence of the father of Henry R. Luce, founder and editor of *Time, Fortune,* and *Life*. And it was the six hundred dollars of this lovely old missionary which had started these institutions.

THOSE PRETTY PICTURES

An old woman was living in Scotland in the most abject poverty. She had never had the advantage of education and had never traveled outside the borders of her own little township. But she had a son who became a sailor and was then traveling to the ends of the earth. Just now he was on the Atlantic someplace, on a ship which was carrying war material to England. However, because of the secrecy of his whereabouts, all she knew was that he was in the United States of America a good deal of the time.

Then the rumors spread around the Scotch village that he had prospered, and the neighbors wondered why that son, who had had a kindly reputation when he was a boy at home, would permit his mother to endure such sufferings. One day one of them ventured to ask the old lady about that son and his apparent negligence.

"Doesn't your son ever send you any money to help you out, Mrs. Robinson?"

"No," reluctantly answered the mother, and yet, eager to defend him from criticism in his own home town, she added eagerly, "but he writes me the most beautiful letters every month—nice long letters telling me all about the United States, its big buildings and trains, airships and theaters—everything. It's a wonderful country. Yes, and he also sends me a pretty picture in almost every letter."

"May I see those pictures?" asked the curious neighbor.

"Why, certainly you may see them. I'm proud to show them to you!" answered the old lady, rising from her rocking chair and going to a nearby shelf.

She reached up to that shelf; got down the old family Bible, which was her constant companion; turned a few pages; and there between the leaves of that old family Bible lay the "beautiful pictures" that her son had been sending her for months from the United States.

What were they? Nothing more nor less than bank notes, each for enough money to keep that old Scotch mother for a month at least.

During all the time of her poverty and need she had that money lying in her Bible hidden away and unused because she did not realize its value. She had, lying there in abundance, riches to satisfy all of her needs.

Need I add much to that simple Scotch story? Need I add that just as that woman had used her Bible to hide all the riches that she needed, so many of us have the abundant riches of that Bible itself to solve the problems of the world, and we let it lie on our tables and our shelves unused and unopened. Jesus said long

16

ago, "I am come that they might have life, and that they might have it more abundantly," and he meant what he said.

❀   ❀

HOW TO REPAY A DEBT

Norman Beasley, one of this nation's great writers, has been a friend of Herbert Hoover for many years and is now engaged in writing the authoritative biography of this great American. One day recently, as I was sitting with him in his home, he told two stories which seem to me to be worth passing on for the general high purpose of helping people to get the most out of life. They are both stories on how to pay back debts we have contracted—and who hasn't faced that particular problem?

When Herbert Hoover was a student in Stanford University, he was a poor boy and had to work his way through college by selling newspapers, running a laundry service, and doing a score of other menial chores. One of them was that of running a concert and lecture course in the college. One day he engaged the great pianist Ignace Jan Paderewski to give a piano concert. He was to pay the famous pianist a certain amount. It rained on the night of his appearance, and there was not enough money in the treasury to pay the pianist. The Polish musician heard about young Herbert Hoover's dilemma and said to him: "Don't worry! I don't want you to lose any money, so we'll just forget my fee."

Years later—say a quarter of a century—Mr. Paderewski was premier of the Polish nation when Herbert Hoover was sent to its starving children with millions of dollars worth of food. He walked into the home of the premier of Poland and said, "Mr. Paderewski, I have come to pay back an old debt. You may not remember it, but many years ago I engaged you to give a piano recital at Stanford University when I was a student. It rained, and we didn't have enough money to pay your fee. You canceled that debt. I am here to pay it back to you today by feeding your women and children."

Mr. Beasley tells me that the great pianist-premier remembered that debt, smiled, and wept a little as this representative of the United States stood before him to pay a college debt. That's one way to pay a debt.

The other way is also illustrated by a Paderewski story which Mr. Beasley told me. It seems that a young American studying music forty years ago in Berlin ran out of funds. Paderewski was in Berlin at the time and heard of this young student's plight, called him in, and lent him money to continue his studies.

One day forty years after that when Paderewski was in Boston, the American, a successful musician walked into his presence and gave him a check to cover every cent he had borrowed, with interest. But Paderewski refused the check, saying: "I don't need it and don't want it. You don't need it now; so why don't you hunt up another music student who is in the same straits that you were in forty years ago in Berlin, and lend it to him? Go find that boy and pass along the help I gave you. That's the best way to pay a debt, my friend!"

❧   ❧

"THE SHOES OF HAPPINESS"

I USED to sit in my home and talk with that wise old poet and philosopher Edwin Markham for hours about his book *The Shoes of Happiness, and Other Poems.* He always replied to my queries about happiness with this stock sentence: "To be happy you have to get rid of *things.*"

His narrative poem "The Shoes of Happiness" tells the story of a king in Istamboul on the Golden Horn who was ill and called his wise men together to ask them to find a cure for his illness.

18

Finally a sibylline crone announced that one thing and one alone would cure him of his illness, and that was to find a man who was perfectly happy and get his shoes for the king to wear.

So the Wise Men searched the world over to find a perfectly happy man.

They went to a rich man, but they found that he was always worrying about his riches and was far from happy. The poor man, they discovered, was always worried about feeding his children. The poet was not the completely happy man, for,

> "No," sighed the poet; "you do me wrong,
> For sorrow is ever the nest of song."

The young were not happy, and the old were not happy.

> The young were restless that youth should stay,
> The old were sad that it went away.

Even the lover was not happy, for he was always worrying about his beloved. Soldiers were not happy, for they were sad for comrades dead. The searchers found a wise man who was a pilgrim and felt certain that they had run across the happy shoes;

> But the pilgrim answered with star-still eyes:
> "I am not glad: I am only wise."

It seemed to be a fruitless search, and they were in despair, for death awaited them back in the palace of the king if they did not bring back the shoes of a happy man.

Then one morning just at dawn they found a tramp lying on the ground. "Laughter lines had scribbled his face," and he was making "sweet sounds from a pipe of willow," singing as he walked along.

Out into the field the searchers ran eagerly and asked for his shoes.

> Your shoes, then, quick, for the great sultan—
> Quick, and all fortunes are yours to choose!

And back came his answer:

19

The happy man, then, according to the implication of that legend, is the man who has rid himself of things. And here is another verse which tells that same story. It is a little waif of a verse I received recently without any apparent parentage:

> There was a time when faith began to slip,
> When I had lost all that I had to lose,
> (Or so it seemed to me)—lost my job,
> My house,
> I had no home, no food, no shoes.
> Then suddenly I felt myself ashamed!
> For I, who talked of shoes,
> Then chanced to meet,
> Upon the busy highway of life,
> A man who had no feet!

ꙅ ꙅ

"I GOT A GLORY!"

ARCHIBALD RUTLEDGE once told a story to a group of radio people in New York City. It was the story of how one day he climbed into a tiny tugboat, which he had often used before to cross a southern river. There was a new Negro engineer in charge of the boat. He sat in the doorway of the engine room reading the Bible.

He was large and fat and squatty. But he was neat, and both his body and his worn blue jeans were clean. Not only that, but as Rutledge started to talk with him he noticed that the engine room itself was immaculate in appearance. The strong odors Rutledge had remembered in that room were gone. The engine itself shone. The brass was gleaming. From under the engineer's seat, all the bilge water which used to be there was

20

gone. Clothes were hanging on the wall on nails instead of being strewn around on the floor and the benches.

When Rutledge asked that fat, stolid Negro engineer how it happened that there was such a change in the boat, the engine room, and the engine itself, that old Negro replied in words which would go far in solving life's most harrassing problems and unhappinesses.

"Mister," he said, looking proudly in the direction of the shining, smooth-running engine, "it's just this way: I got a glory!"

Then Mr. Rutledge added: "Making that engine the finest engine on the river was his glory in life, and having a glory, he had everything."

What a world of wisdom there is in that reply, "I got a glory!"

I know many a mother who has a glory in keeping her humble home neat and clean and her children presentable if not stylish. I know a father who has a glory in working all day to give light and comfort to his children. I know many a teacher who gets entire satisfaction in life out of the glory he has in teaching.

No man or woman can be unhappy, no matter how meager his economic station, who has learned to get a glory out of his work, his home, his friends, and his religion.

ꙅ ꙅ

"OUR KING SAYS, SIR, THERE'S 'OPE AHEAD!"

THESE are bewildering, baffling, uncertain days! With warplanes darkening the skies; with bombs raining down on helpless men, women, and children; with submarines lurking near every sea lane; with ships plunging to their graves beneath the dark, cold waters of many seas; with the danger of devastating diseases and starvation sweeping in the wake of war, who knows which way to turn?

The answer is, "We do!"

Last winter I attended a benefit for English soldiers in Concord, Massachusetts. During the intermissions of that concert several little English refugee children went up and down the aisles selling Christmas cards. There was printed on one of the cards a portion of the address of the King of England in his Christmas broadcast of 1939:

I said to a man who stood at the gate of the year: "Give me a light that I may tread safely into the unknown." And he replied, "Go out into the darkness and put your hand into the hand of God. That shall be to you better than a light and safer than a known way." So I went forth, and finding the hand of God, trod gladly into the night. And He led me towards the hills and the breaking of day in the lone east. May that Almighty Hand guide and uphold us all!

I liked the little English girl who sold me that card. Each time she passed I bought another card just to get a chance to talk with her. She was distinctly cockney. Her hands were red and worn with toil—the marks of washing clothes and scrubbing floors either in her own English home or since she had been in America. She was shy, almost inarticulate, but each time I purchased a card from her I forced her to talk. Her teeth were bad. Her hair was scraggly and a dull color. All that, yes; but ah, her spirit! That was something to make the gods laugh aloud!

I bought a half-dozen of the king's Christmas cards from her just to hear her English cockney brogue. I always asked her how much they were, and she always replied, "A shillin' and ha' penny—a shillin' and ha' penny, sir."

Finally we got so well acquainted that she would smile at me the minute she saw me beckon her over again for some business dealings. Her smile was contagious. I asked her about England and America and her mother and father. Then it happened. Through her tears she said these simple words, pointing as she did so, with a newly acquired American sales technique, to the king's message which she was selling, "Our king says, sir, that there's 'ope ahead!"

That's all she said. But what words they were! Shakespeare

22

could not have said them better! "Our king says, sir, that there's 'ope ahead!"

❂ ❂

A VISIT WITH DAVID LLOYD GEORGE

IT is nine o'clock.

Several thousand men are doing a strange thing in darkened rooms all over America.

These men are members of the Loyal Order of Moose.

What are they doing?

They are praying for little children.

The clocks in a thousand lodge rooms are striking nine. Business and ritual stops. Dancing ceases. Hilarity halts. Heads are bared and bowed. And this is the prayer that those strange fellows called Moose pray unabashed and unashamed:

"Suffer the little children to come unto me, and forbid them not, for of such is the Kingdom of Heaven. And God bless Mooseheart!"

At that same hour hundreds of children in little white night-gowns at the orphanage out in Mooseheart, Illinois—the orphanage which the Loyal Order of Moose maintains—kneel at their bedsides, conscious that their protectors are facing toward Mooseheart. Children and men, facing each other across the hills and fields of night, kneel and pray the same prayer.

I doubt if there is a man who prays that prayer who does not visualize the forms of those little tots kneeling beside their beds. I doubt if there is a man who prays that prayer, taken as it is from the lips of Jesus himself, who is not a better man for that experience. I am told that if a lodge officer forgets that nine o'clock rendezvous with the children at Mooseheart, some member will rise to a point of order and demand that they cease work and go into that sacred ritual.

When did I discover all of this? When I was sent by a news-

23

paper syndicate back in November, 1923, to go with David Lloyd George to visit Mooseheart, near Chicago. There we ate breakfast; there we visited the children; there we watched that sensitive, kindly former Prime Minister of Great Britain bend over those little beds and those children with a pat of the hand and a kindly word for well and ill.

When it was all over, and we were on our way back to the big parade and luncheon in Chicago, he said to a group of us: "That scene I shall never forget in all my life—those children; that great institution. The fact that a lodge of men keeps it up touches me deeply. Two things I wanted to see in Illinois: Lincoln's Tomb and Mooseheart. I have seen one, I shall see the other tomorrow. I shall carry the rich memory of them back to England." And his thin, sensitive, almost woman-like lips trembled as he spoke.

ᕫ   ᕫ

A HERBERT HOOVER EPISODE IN CHINA

BACK in 1920 I was sitting in the palatial home of T'ang Shao-i, in Shanghai, having lunch just before going to the home of Sun Yat-sen for an interview. Mr. T'ang Shao-i was the Chinese patriot's financial backer, and he had arranged that interview through George Sokolsky, an American newspaperman, who was then close to the inner circle of the Chinese Republic.

The 1920 party conventions were then in session in the United States. There was much talk of one Herbert Hoover as a possible candidate on one or both tickets. Nobody seemed to be sure as to whether he was a Democrat or a Republican.

Mr. T'ang Shao-i smiled and said: "He would be a good candidate on either ticket, and he is a friend of China's, so either way we shall be pleased."

Then he told me a thrilling story of the Boxer Rebellion. T'ang Shao-i and two thousand Chinese who were government officials were barricaded in a compound and were being beseiged by the fanatical Boxers, who hated all foreigners and all Chinese who were supposed to be foreign sympathizers. Those marooned foreigners had run out of food and were starving.

One early morning, before daylight had come, a bright-faced, chubby American boy who appeared to be in his late twenties came through a hole in our wall and asked to be brought to me. I was in charge of that barricaded group of refugees. When he came into my room he said: "What do you need most?"

"We need food," I replied.

"All right, I'll get some for you today and bring it in under cover of darkness tonight," replied this young American.

That night he returned with five hundred hams which the Boxers had thrown away because they didn't like the way the foreign devils cured them, and a thousand sacks of flour which he had gotten from the British Legation.

That red-cheeked American boy, an engineer at that time in Tientsin, was Herbert Hoover. And that was the start of his career as Food Administrator.

☽　　☾

"BUT NONE OF THE PHOSPHORESCENCE OF LEARNING"

In his book *New England: Indian Summer* Van Wyck Brooks tells a story about Emily Dickinson, the New England poet, which has given me many a chuckle.

Emily Dickinson was a recluse, a frail, timid person who remained in her own rooms at Amherst adjoining the campus where President Coolidge and Dwight Morrow walked in their day. Emily's day was further back than theirs, but the tradition of her had not died down even when they were there as students.

She dressed in white and moved about the rooms of that old

white house and through the gardens like a wraith. But, in spite of her timidity, she knew all that was going on in that college town and had her own opinions of the personalities who lived in the village and particularly in the college. Her judgments and her phrases which summed them up were biting with sarcasm and often devastating and final.

There was one scholarly person whom she particularly disliked because he had none of the juices of life. The milk of human kindness seemed to have dried up in his soul. He was pedantic, to say the least—dry as bones and dust. Yes, he was a Ph. D., but that was about all. Like many a Ph. D. of today in pulpit, college classroom, and home, he was as dull as a doldrum.

One day Emily Dickinson said of him, "He has all of the facts but none of the phosphorescence of learning."

A good many people are like that. They have a good education, they have all of the facts, but they have none of the sparkle of personality which is necessary to promote any cause, to advance any movement, or to give life a beautiful and a glowing tint. Education and fact-finding are not all of life.

Abraham Lincoln had little education, a so-called "blab school" for a few terms being his only formal schooling. Henry Ford of this generation had only part of a year in grammar school. But each did well in his chosen field. When they started out they had few of the facts of formal schooling, but they had the phosphorescence. They had "It," whatever that is—personality, energy, the eager earnestness to search life and discover its secrets. But more important, each of them had a spirit of service to humanity, an enthusiastic interest in other people. Life is like that. It opens wide doors, not just to those who have had formal educations in the schools and colleges but to those who have the sparkle of personality, the eager desire to do and to serve their fellow men. Life hands more to the personality that has sparkle in its eyes than to the one who has formal learning without the phosphorescence. No human being needs to despair simply because he has not been fortunate enough to have a college education.

REMEMBERING CHRISTOPHER COLUMBUS

My friend Edwin Markham, while visiting in my home in Boston several years ago, was working on a secret poem which he carried about with him mysteriously. He promised he would read it to me when he completed it. On the morning of October 12, he appeared with the poem, which he called "Courage," with the subtitle "Remembering Christopher Columbus."

It is the story of a brave man who fought against great odds, and that is why its author called it "Courage." It has its timely challenge for these days, when we all need to have the faith of our convictions and the courage of our faith.

Mr. Markham's eyes were flashing fire and pride when he came downstairs that morning waving his poem above his long white hair.

"William, here's the poem on that brave explorer. That bird [and that was his word; not mine] had courage and faith!"

Then he proceeded to read that magnificent poem to us at the breakfast table. It is the story of a man who went to the Court of Spain with his dream that the world was round and with the statement that he could find a short path to the Indies:

> He cried even at the court of kings
> His story of incredible things.

When they made fun of him in the Court, Columbus was not baffled; for, as Mr. Markham says,

> He knew he was (his constant boast)
> A servant of the Holy Ghost.

I said to the poet: "Did Columbus actually think that he was called of God to do this important thing?"

"Yes," replied the good gray poet seriously. "I have read every book available, including the Diary of Columbus, and it is clear to me that Columbus looked upon himself as a servant of God on that eventful voyage."

27

Ultimately he got his financial support from the Queen of Spain and started. In this poem there is the story of the long days and nights, the baffled and bewildered sailors, the mutinies; the day the needle seemed to feel some secret jar and also seemed to shake the polar star. His men wanted to turn back, but the sheer courage of Columbus kept them going on into the West. Then came that historic climax—the discovery of the American continent; and Markham ends his poem with these four lines:

> Now let this startling thing be said:
> If land had not been on ahead,
> So mighty had been his gallant dare,
> God's glad hand would have put it there!

I asked the poet what he meant by those concluding lines, and he said: "I mean, William, that God in his heavens, the stars and planets in their courses, the sun and moon and stars, the seasons in their cycles, all history, time and eternity and the very angels in heaven are always on the side of the daring, the audacious, the courageous—the man or woman who catches his vision, feels that he is God's servant, and goes ahead regardless of obstacles!"

What a challenge!

ᕬ   ᕫ

THE KIND OF MAN I WANT TO BE

A SCHOOLTEACHER in a small Illinois town told me a story several years ago. And in repeating that story here I have the feeling that schoolteachers everywhere will be grateful to me, and that it will give them a new pride in their particularly important profession.

In a rural section of Illinois, near Springfield, a young man took a school and worked long hours to do his best by his pupils. He was a man of ideas, and he felt that teaching had opportunities of building character such as no other profession had. The school had had several bad years; teachers had come and gone with too great a frequency. In fact, it seemed that every teacher had been a failure. Not one of them could control the pupils. There seemed to be a lack of discipline, and two of them were actually driven out of the school by unruly boys who delighted in annoying them.

But this particular young man, who had just graduated from the University of Illinois, made up his mind that he would rule by love and friendship instead of by force. Some of the worst of the pupils began to like him and to feel that, after all, maybe there were some teachers who were not the natural enemies of young people. They began to get the feeling that the school was actually organized for their good and their pleasure.

Finally they all got to feeling that way except one big rough farmer boy who was bent on hate and harm and could not be controlled. He ignored all efforts of the new teacher to make friends with him, and not only gloried in his unruly actions but boasted of them to the other pupils. The teacher used all the patience he had and went out of his way to be kind to that boy, but to no avail. The boy seemed bent on mischief—not harmless mischief, but cruel, mean mischief. The teacher finally became discouraged; and at the end of the year he resigned.

The last day of school came late in May. The world was beautiful, as the world can be in Illinois at the end of May with grass springing up, lilacs coming on, the feel of joy and life in the air. But the teacher felt that he had been a failure in not winning that boy. Dejected and discouraged, he went to his room to make out his final reports. He reached into his desk and picked up his books. There on one of the books he saw a piece of paper with a familiar handwriting.

It was the awkward scribble of the boy who had given him the most trouble and whose bad behavior was actually driving him from the school. Inside of that envelope was this note:

Dear Mr. Jones:

I am sorry that I have caused you all the trouble I have this year. It hurts me because you are going away and not coming back. But when I get to be a man, I want to be just like you. Jimmie.

☙   ❧

AUTUMN WOODS

THE man was tired and restless. The jarring radio, with its news of war; the jangle of streetcars; the rumble of trains; the explosions of automobile engines—these were getting him down. He felt that he was on the edge of a nervous breakdown. He was torn with confusion and worry.

Then he walked into the woods with a friend who had noticed his irritability and had persuaded him to take a day off.

They walked for hours in

> The glory that the wood receives
> At sunset in its brazen leaves.

They built a fire, cooked a steak, listened to the whisper of the winds in the trees; and suddenly a sense of peace and quiet came to him.

Oh, the little birds sang east, and the little birds sang west— . . .
And I smiled to think God's greatness flowed around our incomplete-
> ness,—
> Round our restlessness, His rest.

There was the symphony of autumn sounds playing its great orchestral music in the fields and on the hills—the wind in the trees, the sound of running brooks. There was the sound of a quail in a near-by field, and a meadow lark answered the call. Then came the chorus of the crickets a falltime music which stilled his soul.

There were colors which corresponded with the sounds he heard. There was a clump of sumac in crimson bloom. There was the white soft down from milkweed floating in the air. Far away he saw the golden glory of the autumn hills, spread like great Oriental tapestries from every peak and promontory. It was as though every maple tree were on fire with heavenly light. Yellow vines climbed over a stone wall, and there was something restful about the stability of the gray stones and the yellow clinging vines. Clusters of bittersweet ran up the trunk of a tree on the bank of the stream beside which they ate their meal.

Then there was a curve in the little stream where the moss was deep and green. But this was the crowning event of all: He looked into the sky against that crimson sunset and saw a bird flying home to nest! A great sense of quiet and peace fell upon his soul. So quiet was it that, as Bishop Quayle long ago said, "You could have heard the fluttering feather from a Sea Gull's wing as it touched the white-tipped waves of the lake."

❧　　☙

"PULL ON THROUGH"

I AM fortunate in the friendship of Bess Streeter Aldrich, and I have read every book she has ever written. I have talked with her in my own home, and know that she is a fine person.

My favorite of all her books is *Song of Years,* in which she has sturdy old Jeremiah say to this new generation of children: "That's what I always want you children to remember. *Pull yourselves on through.* No matter what you get stuck in . . . mud, swamps, gumbo, snow, jobs, difficulties, disappointments, hurts . . . any hard place or thing in life . . . don't stop like a ox and wait for the blacksnake to crack. Do your own thinkin' . . . your own decidin' . . . then put your neck to the yoke and do your own pullin.' Nobody in this world is ever goin' to help get your load out but yourself. If you forget everything else I ever said to you: *Pull on through.*"

Old Jeremiah gave that group of children sound advice for pioneer days such as his were, or for any other days. We have seen this spirit in many individuals. Madame Curie, ill, cold, weary, even hungry; weakened through lack of food and overwork; with a barn for a laboratory in which to work, struggled through and gave us radium. Alec Templeton in this generation, as did Helen Keller in another generation, pulled on through blindness and physical handicaps which would have stalled less stalwart spirits until each of them became the admiration and wonder of the world. Even the so-called glamor girls did not always have such an easy time of it. Dorothy Lamour worked as an elevator girl in Marshall Field's Store in Chicago and had to wear an unbecoming uniform. Joan Crawford had to wait on table at Stephens College to earn her way to an education. Nor dare we forget that President Roosevelt, stricken in mid-life by infantile paralysis, buckled down and pulled on through.

◌   ◌

WHY VIOLETS HAVE GOLDEN HEARTS

ONCE in the long ago there was a beautiful garden. A strange knight passed through that garden and announced that the king of the garden was coming soon and that he would bring a golden heart to the most beautiful flower.

There was much excitement in the garden at that news. The hollyhocks, white daisies, roses, violets, pansies, hyacinths, poppies, and snowdrops immediately began to primp for the coming of the king of the garden. Each one wanted to be the most beautiful and win the heart of gold.

"Hark! do you hear the footsteps of the king?" asked the snowdrop eagerly of the violet, and the violet nodded that it did. However, it was only an old tired woman walking softly on the earth, crying out: "Oh, you beautiful blossoms! Can you not spare me one?"

"No, no! We can spare none today!" replied the snowdrops. "Go away and come again, for we are saving our blossoms for the king. Ask the violets. They may spare you a few blossoms."

"Yes, indeed," nodded the violets. "We would love to give you some blossoms. Take all you want. Our bed is full—enough for both you and the king!" The old woman stooped to pick some violet blossoms, and her face shone with joy.

The next day a little wounded bird, faint with hunger, fell into the garden near the snowdrops and begged for one tiny seed.

"No, no!" again cried the snowdrops "We have none to spare, for the king is coming, and we must save them all for him."

"Take our seeds!" cried the violets near by. "We have plenty to spare."

So the wounded, hungry bird ate of the violet seeds and was refreshed.

It was night when another visitor came, a crippled frog crying out: "Water! only one drop of water, pretty snowdrops! Your cups are filled with dew. Give me some, or I die of thirst!"

But again the snowdrops shook their pretty heads and turned away crying: "Go away, ugly frog! We need our water to keep our dresses white for the coming of the king."

"Here is some dew from our cups!" cried the violets to the dying frog. "It is fresh and cool and pure. Drink, tired frog, and rest among our cool leaves."

And then a miracle happened. The frog suddenly vanished from sight and in its place stood the king of the garden, clothed in gold and royal purple. In his hands he held a shower of golden hearts, which he scattered among the violets where they lodged lovingly beneath their fragrant petals.

"Yours shall be the golden hearts," cried the king, "for beautiful flowers or beautiful human beings are those who do deeds of loving-kindness the whole day through!" Then, turning to the selfish snowdrops, he said: "Your hearts shall be forever spotted. Footsore and weary, I asked help of you through an old woman; hungry, I came to you through a wounded bird; and thirsty, I came to you through a frog; but you turned me away!"

Just a parable, but one which points the way for all of us in everyday living to get more and more out of life through doing more and more for others.

WHEN TIME IS BLOTTED OUT

THE late Sir James Barrie, Scottish novelist and dramatist, used to tell a story about an ancient monk who wandered into the fields. Suddenly he heard a lark singing in a tree over his head. The monk had never heard a lark sing before, and he stood there entranced until the bird and its song soared off through the heavens in a grand spiral of beauty and sound.

Then he went back to the monastery, and found there a door-keeper whom he did not know instead of the old fellow he had known as intimately as one of his own brothers. He was astonished. But he was even more surprised when the doorkeeper of the monastery did not know him. That doorkeeper looked at the old monk as though he were a complete stranger. He told the doorkeeper his name, but even that was no help.

Finally they looked through the books of the monastery, and those records revealed the fact that there had been a monk of that name there three hundred years or more before that time. For, you see, as the legend has it, "time had been blotted out while he listened to the lark."

I think I know what that legend means. It means that there are some experiences which come to us in life—experiences of tragedy, love, and beauty—which have in them the hint of eternity. Lorado Taft, the famous Chicago sculptor, once said of his art, while he was creating "The Fountain of Time"; "If we sculptors could but learn that the most precious asset of our art is its hint of eternity, we would be better artists. The truly great works of art have an air of serene permanence, the result of mass and simple contour. Destined to live, they smilingly bear in their very structure the guarantee of their immortality. They take one out of time and make him know that he is eternal. When one looks upon a truly great work of art, listens to a great symphony, sees a great painting, reads a great poem or book, time is blotted out for that man and he lives a thousand years in a day."

Some of the everyday experiences of life make different persons out of us, and we grow a century in a night. The carrying of a

34

child; bringing that child into the world; the coming of love; the tragedy of death; hearing great music; a long dark night of anxious waiting by a sickbed; a lost child on a mountainside— these change us, add years to our stature, put the feel of eternity into our souls. Edna St. Vincent Millay felt it once when she was going to a concert and wanted to go alone. She said to her sweetheart,

> Come now, be content.
> I shall be only a little taller
> Than when I went.

❂   ❂

I VISIT DR. SUN YAT-SEN IN SHANGHAI

IT was no small privilege to have spent an afternoon with Dr. Sun Yat-sen back in 1919.

He was in exile, and Japan had a price on his head. They would have executed him on sight. But at that time the French Concession was a haven of refuge for all exiles, and there he lived with Madame Sun Yat-sen, sister of the present Madame Chiang Kai-shek.

When I was ushered into Sun Yat-sen's private library, Mrs. Sun Yat-sen, looking for all the world like a rare piece of Chinese porcelain, brought in tea.

In that conversation Dr. Sun Yat-sen, a slender man, small of stature, with a little black mustache, then streaked with gray, told me of the long fight for Chinese independence and the overthrow of the Manchu Dynasty which was exploiting and throttling China. When Sun Yat-sen's forces finally overthrew the Manchus, Dr. Sun Yat-sen happened to be in Denver, Colorado. One morning at breakfast he picked up the newspapers in the Brown Hotel and saw this headline: "Sun Yat-sen Personally Leads Chinese to Victory." He smiled at the story which followed the headline, for it pictured him carrying a sword and climbing over a small wall, leading his forces to victory. These are the words he used in describing his feelings:

Then I realized that I had to make a momentous decision. Should I take a train west to San Francisco and embark for China to lead my forces personally and consolidate our first victories or should I take a train to New York City and get a ship for England to raise money to continue the revolution?

I looked up trains and ship sailings and discovered that in half an hour I could get a train which would connect with a sailing to England. I took the train and that diversion saved the revolution for the time being, for I got money from England to carry it on. But I have always chuckled over that headline which described me as leading our forces personally, when I was sitting in a Denver Hotel eating my breakfast.

I asked Dr. Sun Yat-sen why he looked to the United States for help, and he gave this answer.

It is because so many of our young men have been trained in your colleges, thanks to the Boxer Indemnity Fund, and because so many of us feel that the United States is our second home. It is because you have sent so many American missionaries to help our people, to teach us, to live with us, to share our problems and sufferings. The very name "America" is a sacred passport to the Chinese heart.

☽   ☾

CO-OPERATING WITH THE INEVITABLE

ONE day in my Southern home I was talking with an old Negro man, who has done chores for the white people in Moundsville for a quarter of a century or more. And all during that time he has never had much more than the bare necessities of life—enough to eat and a meager, even leaky, roof over his woolly old head. I doubt if Uncle Mose ever went to a picture show in all his life. Such luxuries are simply not within the scope of his budget. I doubt if he ever had a dish of ice cream in his life. Uncle

36

Mose has all he can do to get potatoes and now and then on Sundays a little meat for his large brood of children.

He has always had what seemed to our town a lot of bad luck. He has lost three children by accident. He has had two shacks to burn. He lives on the river's edge, and about every two years the floods come and sweep away his garden. Lately he has lost his wife. This summer when I went to see him I said to him, "Uncle Mose, you always seem so happy. I never saw you that you didn't smile or laugh or tell a funny story. And yet you have had more trouble than anybody in this town. Don't you ever worry?"

"Worry? I leaves dat to you white folks. As fer me, I has learned to co-operate wid de inevitable."

I have been thinking a lot about what Uncle Mose told me. Most of us run into things which we cannot change. There are certain inevitables of life, and if we could only learn to adjust ourselves to them we would be happier. I don't mean that we have to succumb supinely to any fate that overtakes us. I mean that when we run into something that is unavoidable we should learn to turn to something else and do the best we can.

Recently, after a quarter of a century, I have been rereading *Mrs. Wiggs of the Cabbage Patch.* Mrs. Wiggs had the right attitude toward life, for she once said to a friend:

"I believe in gittin' as much good outen life as you kin—not that I ever set out to look for happiness; seems like the folks that does that never finds it. I jes' do the best I kin where the good Lord puts me at, an' it looks like I got a happy feelin' in me 'most all the time."

ꙮ   ꙮ

THREE WORDS OF STRENGTH

I HAVE often wanted to conduct a contest in which all of us would select the ten most beautiful words in the English language, just as we all like to select the "Ten Most Important Men of the Nation," "The Ten Best-Dressed Women in the World," or "The Ten Significant Books of All Time."

But in lieu of doing that I am going to allow Friedrich von Schiller to select for us the three most important words of all time as he sees them—at least the three great words of strength, as he calls them:

> There are three lessons I would write,
> Three words as with a burning pen,
> In tracings of eternal light
> Upon the hearts of men.

The first word that Schiller selects is *Hope*. And in selecting it he but echoes an old phrase from Greek days, "Keep ever shining before thy vagrant footsteps the kindly light of hope." We need to make that word an integral part of our thinking and of our vocabulary.

> Have hope. Though clouds encircle round,
> And gladness hides her face in scorn;
> Put off the shadow from thy brow;
> No night but hath its morn!

The second word is *Faith*. We need that too. We need faith in the divine rule of this universe.

> Have Faith. Where'er thy bark is driven—
> The calm's disport. The Tempest's mirth—
> Know this: God rules the hosts of heaven,
> The inhabitants of earth!

And Schiller's third word in the list is *Love*. That word seems to be an outmoded word these days when we see hate and hurt running rampant around the earth. But love still lives, and love is still one of the words of strength, as Schiller calls it.

> Have Love. Not love alone for one,
> But man, as man, thy brother call;

And scatter like a circling sun,
Thy charities on all!

Hope, faith, and love, and the greatest of these is love!

⋆   ⋆

"YOU'VE GOT TO GET IT INSIDE"

NOT long ago I heard a foreign missionary speak in Concord, Massachusetts. He has been, for years, Chiang Kai-shek's adviser in international affairs and has lived in the generalissimo's home for months at a stretch. He undoubtedly knows more about the intimate life of the great Christian general than any other person.

He told us a lot of interesting things about the home life of the general—how he has a half-hour of prayer, Bible reading, and meditation from seven o'clock to half-past seven each morning before he even eats his breakfast—how in that half-hour of meditation he reads the Bible. It is his desire to translate the Bible for the Chinese and to print a Bible with the sayings of Moses and the Hebrew prophets parallel with the great sayings of the Chinese sages and prophets; for he feels that a revelation of God's will for humanity came through the Chinese sages as well as through the Hebrew prophets.

One day his young wife, a graduate of Wellesley College, in America, went into the general's room and found him repeating to himself the words of the twenty-third Psalm. She asked him why he was memorizing it. He answered: "Because it fits the needs of my soul in these dark days when we are going through the valley of death. I like the Psalms. They are the great classics of all literature, and I have memorized thirty of them already."

"But why memorize them when you have them in the Bible to read every day?" his young wife asked.

"Why memorize them? Because you ought to have those Psalms

inside of your soul; not outside. Then you can carry them with you into councils of war, onto the battlefields, in every crisis of life. They ought to be inside of you!"

That story reminded me of a question I once asked a French chef. I said to him: "Why put the seasoning in the food while it is cooking and not on top of it, or outside of it after it is cooked?"

He replied: "we put the seasoning in the food while it is cooking and not on top of it, or outside of it after it is cooked. We get it inside of the food."

Both Chiang Kai-shek and the French chef are right. It is what we get inside of us that counts. If we have great poetry, great Bible quotations, great thoughts on the inside of our minds and hearts we will always have them with us in times of darkness.

ᴐ　　ᴑ

SPRING WILL COME

A BOY about nine years of age was out riding with his mother on Palm Sunday afternoon after having attended a very beautiful service in the morning. As they passed through the fields and woods outside the city, the boy noticed the buds on the trees beginning to swell and the grass turning green. He asked his mother how the trees and grass knew when it was time for them to come out—what told them. The mother explained to him that it was a sort of resurrection that God brought about each year, and drew some simple lessons of how God, through his universal laws, has promised to bring us back into full immortal life after we leave this world. Dick was very deeply impressed and asked innumerable questions.

That evening when he was ready for bed he brought up the subject again. The mother talked to him again about God and his universal laws of death and life, of mortality and immortality. She told him how God pours his blessings on the world through springtime and how he pours his blessings on human beings.

She made mention of the barren prairies of the west, through which they had driven the preceding summer on their vacation. She told him that human lives would be as barren as those desert stretches if we did not accept God and open our hearts to his laws and blessings which he so freely offers us.

Dick lay in his bed, silent for a few moments, and then he said: "Mother, I guess God knows his business. We'd better stick to him, hadn't we?"

"Yes," the mother replied, seeing that an eternal truth was seeping through.

"I guess I'd better say my

> Now I lay me down to sleep,
> I pray thee, Lord, my soul to keep,

and then go to sleep and leave things to him, hadn't I?"

"I guess you had better, Son. That's the wisest way."

"I guess God will take care of everything in the long run, won't he, Mother?"

"What do you mean, Dick?" asked that mother, curious to know what was working in his boyish mind.

"I mean it's like spring coming—those buds we saw swelling on the trees today and the grass turning green—and how God makes the dry and barren prairies like gardens in his own time. I guess that's what is happening in the world. Spring will come, for God's still on the job! I guess I won't worry! I guess I'll just go to sleep and leave things to him, eh, Mother?"

ꙅ   ꙅ

"IT HELPS, IF YOU'RE GOING IN THE RIGHT DIRECTION"

I was sitting in the stadium at Harvard watching a Harvard-Yale football game. Harvard won the toss. The wind was blowing a terrific gale in the direction of the kickoff. I said to a friend: "There's a hard wind blowing today."

"But it helps, if you are going in the right direction," my friend replied. "And Harvard is going in the right direction."

My friend was right, for the wind literally lifted that kickoff into the air and carried it high and far beyond the goal posts. Also, every time that Harvard punted, the wind seemed to be with them and added twenty yards to each kick.

As I sat there watching that game I said to myself: "That is true of life in general: There's a strong wind blowing today and it helps, if you're going in the right direction. How it helps!"

Those of us who use the airplanes now and then remember a bit of the vernacular of pilots. They talk of "tail winds" and tell of how "We'll make a fast trip today from Chicago to Kansas City, for we have a tail wind blowing." That means that the wind is behind the plane, helping it along faster than it would go under its own powerful momentum and its tremendous engines.

Several years ago Paul Hutchinson, one of the editors of *The Christian Century*, said to me: "There are great social ideas loose in the world today, and ideas do not die with their progenitors. Whether we like it or not, the thing that is happening in Russia will happen to all the world in one form or another."

Paul Hutchinson was right. There is a strong wind of social reforms, even of revolutionary social change, blowing today, and it helps, if you are going in the right direction. The vital thing for all of us as individuals to do in these days is to keep our thinking headed toward the future—toward social justice, toward the dawn of a new world, for it is coming as surely as the sunrise. The winds are blowing in that direction.

One windy day in the Yellowstone Park I watched an eagle flying in the deep canyon of that beautiful abyss. It looked as if the winds would sweep the eagle to its death against the cliff. But that wise old eagle knew his winds. He intuitively spread his wide wings and let himself be lifted and carried above those sheer cliffs on the sweep of the winds.

Yes, there's a strong wind blowing today, and it helps, if you are going in the right direction.

೨   ೧

"BEAUTY IS WHERE YOU FIND IT"

NOT long ago I picked up the *Christian Science Monitor* and found a piece entitled "Beauty Is Where You Find it." It was an article about—of all things—weeds. The idea intrigued me, for in our own home we have always made household bouquets out of weeds, tall slender grasses of the field, moss, lichen, and goldenrod.

It seems that out in Pasadena a group of women inaugurated the first "Weed Show" in all history. It was an instant hit, and people who went to the show were astonished at the beauty achieved with a vase of weeds and grasses.

These women made an important discovery in their weed show. They discovered that some things which are looked upon as weeds in one state are looked upon as flowers in another. Queen Anne's lace, for instance, a common weed of New England, is a choice flower in California. The early summer goldenrod, which is a weed in New England, is a garden flower in California. The Kansas gay-feather, which is a weed in the Midwest, is a garden flower in New England. The steeplebush, meadowsweet, meadow rue, and common dock make beautiful table decorations.

A story Dr. F. B. Meyer, of England, once told comes to my mind as I think of this first weed show in California. Dr. Meyer had been shown a wonderful collection of chrysanthemums, and the gardener said to him: "All these glorious blooms come from the daisy, the outcast field daisy."

"I see!" said Dr. Meyers. "A chrysanthemum is a field daisy, plus man?"

"Yes," said the gardener, "that is it."

"And," added the minister, "a Christian is a common man, plus God!"

Luther Burbank proved that a weed is a flower, plus man. He did this with the common field daisy, which was much despised by farmers in the East. Mr. Burbank said to me one day that he first took an interest in that outcast weed because "every man's hand seemed to be against it."

Then he told what he had done with it: "I crossed it with a Japanese daisy and an English daisy and produced the Shasta daisy. The bloom of my Shasta daisy has grown as much as two feet in circumference and seven inches from tip to tip. It will grow anywhere out of doors where the cold will not kill an oak tree, and when cut it will last six weeks. I also took the despised Arizona Desert Cactus and bred out of it its poison and all of its spikes and made it edible for horses and cattle. It is my theory that there are no outcasts in nature; everything has a use, and everything in nature is beautiful if we are eager to ennoble it. Every weed is a possible beautiful flower."

So is it with human beings. When I remember what Luther Burbank told me about redeeming the outcasts of nature I add to that the headline of this newspaper story, "Beauty Is Where You Find It," and go on my way rejoicing.

ᴐ　　ᴒ

WINGS FOR WORMS

Mr. Luther Burbank used to tell me that doing wrong was a bad bargain. He used to say with a twinkle in his eyes: "Doing harm to a plant or a child taking advantage of a neighbor in a business deal, being unkind to animal or human, cheating in friendship or marriage—what you call 'sin'—narrows itself down to being a bad bargain."

I had never heard the matter of what my parents called "sin" put in that light before. Then Mr. Burbank told me a simple story out of his own particular interests which I have never forgotten.

Here is the story as he told it:

Once upon a time there was a skylark flying with its father on a lovely bright morning right here in Santa Rosa.

That skylark's daddy was telling him what fine birds skylarks were, to show the little chap that he came of a worthy lineage, of a fine family. Skylarks could fly higher and sing more sweetly than any other bird.

But that little skylark had one ear to the ground, and far below him he could see a man walking along through a field and could hear the tinkle, tinkle, tinkle of a bell. So down that baby skylark shot, for that is the way skylarks fly. They soar in spirals, but they drop like plummets when they go down. When he got down to the field he found a queer little man driving a red cart, and the man cried out: "Earthworms for sale. Earthworms traded for skylark feathers! Earthworms for skylark feathers!"

The little skylark loved earthworms. The mere thought made his mouth water, so he called out in musical words: "How many worms do you give for a feather?"

"Two worms for a single feather!" said the queer little man, so the young skylark plucked two feathers and traded. When he had gobbled up the worms he flew back into the sky to join his father, hoping that his father would not notice the absence of two feathers in his bright plumage. His father was still talking about what fine birds skylarks were and did not notice.

The next day that little skylark listened for the bell and traded a feather for two more earthworms. He did this day after day. Then one day he made a bargain with the queer little man and traded five feathers for ten worms. "It's a deal!" said the little man.

And so it went, day after day. But on the twentieth day, when the baby skylark lifted his wings, he could not fly. He was tied to earth and finally was killed. So, after that, all the skylarks gathered each spring around the foolish skylark's grave, and the elder skylarks told of how that foolish skylark sold its wings for worms.

It's a simple tale, with an echo in it of an ancient biblical wisdom about a man who sold his birthright for a mess of pottage. Mr. Burbank chuckled as he told me that story, he who loved children so much and had a collection of such stories. But I have never forgotten it.

❧   ❧

THE MISER OF MARSEILLES

DURING World War I, when I spent a year in France, I traveled around that nation a good deal. During a long stay in the city of Marseilles I ran across an interesting legend of how, years ago, there was an old man who used to walk the streets of that seaport town whom they called "The Miser of Marseilles." He was an object of derision throughout the whole city and even throughout the south of France, for everybody seemed to know him.

Apparently he loved nothing and had no other object than to hoard every bit of money he got hold of; for what purpose, none knew. He was hated and was hooted whenever he appeared on the streets. When he died, he was so despised that only a single person attended his funeral. Then his will was read, and these were its strange terms:

From my infancy I noticed that the poor people of Marseilles had great difficulty in getting water. I noticed that water, the gift of God, was very dear and difficult to obtain. And when they could get that water, it was not as pure and clean as God intended it to be.

Therefore I vowed before God that I would live but for one purpose, for one end. I would save money, money, money; that I might give it to the city on one condition: that an aqueduct be built to bring fresh, pure water from yonder lake in the hills to Marseilles. That I now make possible by leaving all my hoarded wealth to this city. This is my last will and testament.

That aqueduct is one of the historic sights which guides and natives point out to visitors above all other things. Travelers in Marseilles today hear the poor people say as they drink the pure, sweet water from the lake in the hills, "Ah, when the miser died we misunderstood him, but he did it all for us! We called him

46

the miser of Marseilles, but he was more than that; he was the saviour of Marseilles."

If we human beings could but learn the one inescapable meaning of that parable we would know the secret of how to get the most out of life which is to give the most to life.

If we parents could but learn that every child in our care is a possible benefactor of mankind; a possible research worker who may discover the cure for cancer; a possible Dr. Banting or Dr. Best who may grow up to find the control of diabetes; a possible saviour of the nation in some future time of crisis; we would have more respect for the personalities of our children. If we could but learn that a Negro child might be an incipient Dr. Carver, a Booker T. Washington, Paul Robeson, Countee Cullen, or Paul Laurence Dunbar!

☙   ❧

STARS, DIVINING RODS, AND SPRINGS

Oliver Wendell Holmes, Jr., who later became the "Father of Modern Jurisprudence," as Lord Haldane of England called him, was born on March 8, 1841. He was wounded in the Civil War, was made Associate Justice of our Supreme Court in 1902, and remained a member of that august body until he retired at the age of 91, in 1932.

When he was born back in 1841, his father, the famous poet Oliver Wendell Holmes wrote to his sister telling of the birth of his son and said: "He may some day be a member of Congress, or a president of the United States, but just at this moment he is scratching his face and sucking his right forefinger."

On the celebration of Oliver Wendell Holmes, Jr.'s, one hundredth anniversary a law library surrounded by a beautiful rose garden was dedicated in his honor. That library and garden were paid for with a strange bequest. When Justice Holmes died in

1935, two days before his ninety-fourth birthday, he left an estate of about a half million dollars and, of all unusual things, he left it to the United States of America. Nobody knows why this fun-loving, wise man left his money to his government, but the gesture was in keeping with his life.

He once said to a group of men: "No man has earned the right to intellectual ambition until he has learned to lay his course by a star he has never seen; to dig by the divining rod for springs he may never reach."

When I read that bludgeoning sentence I thought of some of the great of the earth; I thought of a man named Moses, who stood on a mountain peak and looked down into a Promised Land that he was never able to enter, but who, for long years of his life, had steered by that star for the people he so nobly led through the wilderness for forty years.

I thought of Percival Lowell, the Harvard astronomer, who spent years in calculating the location of a new planet, later to be discovered and named Pluto in his honor. Those calculations were so real to him that he named the exact spot in the skies where Pluto would be found. He raised money and built an observatory near Flagstaff, Arizona, where he did the mathematical work for the discovery of Pluto ten years before there was photographic equipment powerful enough to photograph it. He died several years before it was actually discovered. If ever a man steered by a star he could not see and dug with a divining rod for springs he would never reach it was Percival Lowell.

ᕲ   ᕱ

"I HAVE AN UNDERSTANDING WITH THE HILLS"

GRACE HAZARD CONKLING once wrote a little poem called "After Sunset," and I have always felt that she should have called that poem by its first line:

48

I have an understanding with the hills
At evening when the slanted radiance fills
Their hollows, and the great winds let them be,
And they are quiet and look down at me.

It is a good thing to have an understanding with the hills, especially in these turbulent, tumultuous days of uncertainty. The Psalmist of old had such an understanding when he sang, "I will lift up mine eyes unto the hills, from whence cometh my help."

The Psalmist knew that the water which fed the dry valleys in which he lived came from those far hills; that the very health and vitality of his existence came from their richness; that those hills, when storms blew from the west, protected that valley from the onsweep of those storms.

Years ago I lived in San Francisco, and I used to go out on my back porch and look at old Mount Tamalpias across the bay, Oakland way. It was always there. I came to feel that Mount Tamalpias was my friend. It seemed like some stalwart sentinel out of Eternity, as indeed it was.

When I was worried about contemporary things—earthquakes, fires, unhappiness, personal affairs, disturbances of earth and sky and sea; of home and business and city—I would go out and look at Old Tamalpias, and it gave me a sense of steadiness, peace, security, and quiet. It was so still and sure of itself under the morning sun or the starlit skies of night. I could always see it. No, not always, for on some days the fog rolled in from the Pacific through the Golden Gate, and even old Tamalpias was hidden from my sight. Sometimes when it rained I could not see Tamalpias. Sometimes on a dark night it was hidden from me.

However, I never doubted that it would be there—that it *was* there. I knew that when the fog rolled away, when the darkness departed, when the rain ceased, my old friend Mount Tamalpias would be there. It had never failed me. I had "an understanding with the hills."

So we have a right to expect that when the fog, rain, and darkness of these present war days pass away, as pass they will, the eternal things—all of the things really worth while—will still be standing: Home, love, faith, truth, the church, dreams, idealism, friendship, and religion will still be standing, and we shall all of us still have "an understanding with the hills."

☙   ❧

RADIATING PERSONALITY

EVER since I read the vitalic story of the life of the Curies written by Eve Curie I have been fascinated with the penetrating and healing properties not only of radium but of personality.

I remember spending a day in the New England Deaconess Hospital in Boston, where they have one of the largest supplies of radium in the world. They gave me a demonstration of its powers. They hid a piece of radium in a sealed tube and then allowed me to put my ear to a radio contrivance. I could hear the vibrant sound of the radiations of that radium. It sounded like the noise of an automobile engine running in high. That is the modern way of discovering the whereabouts of lost radium, they told me. Following this, they told me fantastic stories of radium that had been thrown into toilets and ash cans, of how they take that machine and carry it into a sewer or an ash heap and invariably discover their priceless lost radium.

And just as a bit of radium will throw off particles of itself without exhausting itself perceptibly, we human personalities throw off invisible vibrations of ourselves. Almost without knowing it we throw off invisible vibrations from our spirits which either depress or brighten the lives of others. We go forth in love, in hate, in indifference, in wrath, in coldness, in good cheer and good humor, or in gloom and sorrow.

Without our even speaking, dogs and other animals know when we love them. These emotional radiations come to us and go out from us continually, just as the particles of power go out from radium. If we keep constantly aware of that fact we shall be more apt to keep our emotions under control and make a definite attempt to send out the healing radiations of love, kindliness, and good will to those we meet every day.

The radiations of radium will not pass through lead, but the radiations of a lovable and loving personality will pass through anything. What we think and feel determines what we are and what we radiate.

I have noticed this so much in our relations with animals. It is a well-known fact that the thing which we radiate—kindness, fear, or ill will—largely determines the way even a dog responds to us. Even a ferocious dog will respond to calmness, lack of fear, a quiet voice, and a friendly pat. The "Seeing Eye" dogs teach us this.

But this response is especially noticeable in children. One day this summer Mrs. Stidger and I undertook the task of keeping our two grandchildren, Billy, aged two, and Jacky, aged three, for a week. We were both "punch drunk" the first day. Mrs. Stidger was what any man would call slightly irritated by the end of the day. Both of us, conscious of our frayed nerves, were trying to hide it from the children. But late that evening Jacky said to me, after a slight display of that irritation on the part of Mrs. Stidger "Nanna will eat you up, Da, if you don't go away!" He had sensed something. Children are as sensitive as seismographs to the radiations of their elders.

꩜   ꩜

"SOME GAY, ADVENTUROUS, LOVELY THING"

MY friend Grace Noll Crowell has written a beautiful poem which starts off like this:

> The day will bring some lovely thing:
> I say it over each new dawn:

51

Some gay, adventurous thing to hold
Against my heart when it is gone.

Then she goes on to tell us what each new day may bring of joy, adventure, and delight—"some sudden beauty without name"; such as a snatch of song, a breath of pine in the woods, a poem lit with sudden flame, high tangled bird notes, some sudden misty purple bloom, or a late line of crimson sun. And then she finishes her poem with these two lines:

Each night I pause, remembering
Some gay, adventurous, lovely thing.

When I read that beautiful poem I remembered a family tradition. Betty and I used to have what we called "One Adventure Each Day" when she was a child. From the time Betty was four years of age we went out, deliberately seeking our one adventure each day. We did not wait for that adventure to come to us.

I remember some of them this morning as I write. Sometimes it was walking across the fields and finding an old tree with a huge girth, a tree which had stood a hundred years or more. We put our arms around that tree, patted its trunk, and tried to remember the adventurous things it had seen in its long life—Indians, pioneers, storms, hurricanes. It was great fun. Often our adventure would be helping an old lady across the city street or buying up the remaining newspapers that a newsboy had not sold and selling them ourselves. When we didn't sell them all to passers-by we would take them home and try to sell them to mother, a matter which we never wholly achieved. Other days, we would deliberately walk across a snowy field instead of walking around it on a well-cleared path which had been made for us; thus pretending that we were pioneers. Wading thigh deep in snow was much more fun than walking over well-cleared paths. Many times we took crippled, hungry, or lost dogs home and nearly always got into trouble with Mrs. Stidger. But on at least two occasions we were permitted to keep dogs "until their owners claimed them." But no owner claimed one of them, and "Atta Boy" was a household fixture for two years—a big, friendly, faithful police dog, who evidently got lost. Once we brought a lost child home, fed it, and later called the police and found its home. We still talk with warm hearts about that adventure in our family circle.

Yes, this "One Adventure Each Day" is a glorious thing, even if it is only a sunrise, a sunset, a starlit night, finding the first flowers of spring, the last fluttering crimson leaf of fall or the first snow flakes drifting down past the window.

> And so I rise and go to meet
> Each day with wings upon my feet.

❧　☙

A SALUTE

DR. CAMDEN M. COBERN was one of America's finest preachers. He later became a teacher in Allegheny College in Meadville, Pennsylvania, and an archaeologist who excavated with Petrie in Egypt and Babylonia. One of his books on this subject has become a classic in its field.

One of the most dramatic stories I ever heard about a father in wartime I heard about Dr. Camden M. Cobern, this Chicago preacher.

It was in the first World War. He was in his sixties, but the spirit of adventure was still in his soul, and someway he managed to have himself sent to France to speak to the boys in the camps. He was too old to go, but the Red Cross needed an eloquent man badly, and he was certainly eloquent. Also he had known what it meant to endure hardship during the days of his explorations in Egypt, sleeping in tents and roughing it as archaeologists necessarily had to do. In any case they sent him to France.

One cold wintry day, with the wind blowing sleet and snow in his face, this old man was trudging down a French road on his way to address a camp of American boys ten miles from his post.

There was no transportation available for him, so he decided to walk it. After five miles he was worn out and wet with snow. His eyeglasses were covered with water, and his vision dimmed. Suddenly he heard the sound of horses' hoofs on the cobbled stones of the French road. He looked up and saw advancing toward him a company of cavalry, which took up the whole of the narrow road. He saw that unless the company of horsemen divided and let him through he would have to go down into one of those deep ditches filled with water which were on either side of the road. He had great respect for those American soldiers, so he made up his mind as that company of cavalry got nearer and nearer, with the young captain riding his horse like a ramrod, that he would give the captain his best salute and step down into the ditch to let them pass without breaking the ranks.

As they got within ten feet, Dr. Cobern raised his weary shoulders, lifted his hand to a stiff salute, and started for the ditch. But suddenly he stopped dead still. The young captain was sliding from his horse without any effort at discipline or dignity, and, as he slid down, he was crying out: "Dad! Dad! Dad!"

And in a few seconds that company of cavalry watched their captain gather into his arms the weary form of his own father. For Captain Camden M. Cobern Jr. was that boy's name.

☽   ☾

GET THE GLARE OUT OF YOUR EYES

A GENTLEMAN was invited by an artist of some fame to come to his studio and see a painting he had just finished.

He went at the appointed time and was shown by an attendant into a dark room and left there. He sat in the room alone for fifteen minutes before his artist friend came for him and took him to see the new painting.

Before he left the studio the artist said: "I suppose you thought it queer to be left in that dark room so long?"

"Yes," the visitor replied, "I did."

"Well," said the artist, "I knew that if you came into my studio with the glare of the street in your eyes you could not appreciate the fine colorings of the painting. So I left you in a dark room till the glare had worn out of your eyes."

That experience reminds me of a friend of mine who wrote to John Oxenham during the first World War and asked him to tell the story of the composition of one of his most beautiful poems. In answer Mr. Oxenham told of the tragic day when he received a telegram from the War Department with a message which every parent constantly feared—"Killed in Action!" It was his own son. Bewildered, he walked alone, hardly knowing what to do, barely knowing where he went. He came at last to a little London chapel. He went in. There in its semidarkness he sat until peace stole into his soul again—the peace of God in that worshipful place—and the glare had left his eyes and heart. And there he penned the lines of a poem which has since that time become a hymn:

> Mid all the traffic of the ways—
> Turmoils without, within—
> Make in my heart a quiet place,
> And come and dwell therein:
>
> A little shrine of quietness,
> All sacred to thyself,
> Where thou shalt all my soul possess,
> And I may find myself.

Yes, all of us, especially city dwellers, need each day to find some quiet dark place where we may get the glare, the noise, tumult and confusion out of our eyes and souls. It may be that we shall have a quiet room in our homes, a nook in the woods, the shadow of a hill, some quiet cathedral or church where we may go for a few minutes. It takes just that experience to get the glare out of our eyes and the tumult out of our souls so that we may appreciate the delicate colors of life's great art.

MAKE IT BRIEF

A PREACHER friend of mine was talking to me about these stories and asked me how I managed to make them so short. He wasn't used to that in sermon construction.

Then I told him a story I had just heard. It was about a mutual minister friend of ours who showed up one day with a bandaged finger. A lay parishioner of his said: "Frank, how did you cut your finger?"

The preacher replied: "I was shaving and got to thinking about my sermon and cut my finger, Jim."

The layman replied: "Well, the next time, Frank; you get to thinking about your finger and cut your sermon."

The layman was right. Brevity is not only the soul of wit, but it is the soul of conversation, letters, and anything worth while. Horace Greeley, one of the nation's great pioneer editors, once said: "I would write shorter editorials, but I haven't time."

The classic story about brevity is told by an old journalist. A certain beginner in journalism picked up what seemed to him to be a great story. He hurried to the telegram office and queried the editor of his newspaper. "Column story on big murder—shall I send it?"

The answer came back: "Send six-hundred words."

To this the enthusiastic cub replied: "Can't be told in less than twelve hundred words."

Then came this reply: "Story of creation of world told in six hundred words. Try it."

This fits in with the spirit of Joel Chandler Harris, editor of the *Atlanta Constitution* and creator of "Uncle Remus," who in his advice to writers for the daily press once said in my presence:

When you've got a thing to say,
Say it! Don't take half a day.
When your tale's got little in it,
Crowd the whole thing in a minute!
Life is short—a fleeting vapor—
Don't you fill the whole blamed paper

56

With a tale which, at a pinch,
Could be cornered in an inch!
Boil her down until she simmers.
Polish her until she glimmers.
When you've got a thing to say,
Say it! Don't take half a day.

❂   ❂

WAS IT WORTH WHILE?

MANY years ago in a little village in Wales a widowed mother, who was very poor, tried to keep her small family together by working. One day her baby boy took seriously ill. In spite of the fact that it was ten miles to the nearest doctor, that Welsh mother walked every step of the way.

When she arrived at the doctor's home and told him the story, the doctor did not know whether to go or not. It would be a long, hard trip and he dreaded it. Also, he knew that he would not receive any fee, for the mother was too poor. He said to himself that it would make little difference whether that boy's life was saved or not, for if he died it would only be one less mouth for that poor mother to feed. Even if the boy lived he would only grow up to be another common laborer.

In other words, the doctor was rationalizing his inner desire to avoid that duty. He knew he ought to go, but he kept asking himself: "Is it worth while?"

Finally that mother's pathetic earnestness and the fact that she herself had walked those ten miles made him ashamed not to go. After all, the average doctor does have a conscience about these things. Few doctors will actually turn down a need just because they do not see a fee in sight. The real doctor does an immense amount of work for nothing. I have never lived in a city where doctors have not always been ready to do any work that I suggested for the poor and needy.

Well, this Welsh doctor finally decided to take the ten-mile trip. About the year 1923, I saw that little boy. He was in America, and I went to Chicago and Mooseheart to interview him when he visited the home for children that the Moose Lodge supports. His name was, and is, David Lloyd George, former Prime Minister of Great Britain. He is the little boy who might have died if that doctor had given a negative answer to his inner query, "Is it worth while to make that hard trip?"

GOOD MEN AND BAD?

SEVERAL years ago I was visiting Mrs. Joaquin Miller, wife of the California poet, up on "The Hights" near Piedmont which Miller had built with his own hands. It is one of the truly unique literary shrines of the nation, for he built a house for each member of his family and no other member dared enter that house save on the special invitation of the owner. That was his way of illustrating the sacredness of one's individuality. He also built stone memorials there to Dante, Frémont, the California explorer, Goethe, and Schiller. It was his life long habit to take into his home the outcasts of the Bay States and give them shelter. On "The Hights" he had a private burial ground, where those who had no friends could be buried with proper comradeship. He was a unique man as well as a great poet, best known, perhaps, for his poem on Columbus entitled "Sail On! Sail On!"

But to me the poet is best known for a bit of human philosophy which Mrs. Miller and I accidently discovered one day on one of my visits to "The Hights" overlooking Oakland Bay, on the Piedmont Hills.

Mrs. Miller permitted me to rummage through his unpublished manuscripts. One day I found a little poem which read like this:

> In men whom men condemn as ill
> I find so much of goodness still,

> In men whom men pronounce divine
> I find so much of sin and blot,
> I *hesitate* to draw the line
> Between the two, where God has not.

Excited, I called Mrs. Miller in and read that poem to her. She had a strange look in her eyes as she turned to her own desk and took out a piece of yellow paper. Then she turned to me and said: "There's an interesting story connected with that poem, which was one of Joaquin's best-known verses. He wrote that version when he was a young man shortly after we were married. But twenty years later as he lay, covered with an old buffalo robe, on that very bed where you are sitting, he changed one word in that poem. When he had made this change he called me in and said: "When I wrote that poem about condemning and judging I was immature. Now, after a quarter of a century has passed and I have learned more with the wisdom of experience, I want it to read this way, with just one word changed:

> In men whom men condemn as ill
> I find so much of goodness still,
> In men whom men pronounce divine
> I find so much of sin and blot;
> I DO NOT DARE to draw the line
> Between the two, where God was not."

All that Joaquin Miller had done was to change "hesitate" to "do not dare." And, to my way of thinking, that was a tremendous change which the wisdom of the years had taught the poet.

Who of us does dare to draw the line; who dares to assume the omnipotent power to judge a fellow man? What husband dares to judge a wife; what wife to judge a husband; what friend to condemn and judge another?

ॐ   ভ

HOW TO MEND CHRIST'S SHOES

THERE is a beautiful legend of an ancient saint who went into the desert to live in solitude so that he could perfect his soul by denying himself and living apart from humanity. His name was Saint Anthony. Finally this saint became very much satisfied with himself and his soul.

"Most certainly there is no holier saint than I, and no living man serves God better than I!"

But even at that very instant of his spiritual egotism he heard a voice, which he knew to be the voice of God, saying: "No, Anthony, thou art not the best servant of God. There is one even more saintly than you."

"Where does this man live, Lord, so I may visit him and learn from him?"

"He lives in Jerusalem!" replied the Lord, "and they call him Cobbler Conrad."

"What does he do that I do not do?" asked St. Anthony.

"Go and discover for yourself what he does that you do not do," replied the Lord.

So Anthony took up his staff and his few belongings and started for Jerusalem. When he arrived he sought out the humble shop of Conrad the Cobbler and found him in his meager surroundings pounding away on a pair of shoes. Without even getting up from his bench he smiled a greeting to Anthony and asked what he wanted done.

Then Anthony said: "What have you done that the Lord looks upon you as a greater saint than I am?"

"I have done little," replied Conrad the Cobbler," but just sit here and mend the shoes that are brought in to me. But I mend each pair of shoes and sandals as though each belonged to Christ himself. I mend them as I would for him, my Saviour. That is all I do. That may not be much."

Then Saint Anthony bowed his head humbly and departed, going back to his desert tent with a more humble spirit. That night in his prayers he said: "Now, I see, Lord God. I have set up myself as a saint. But Conrad sees something of Christ in every man, woman, and child. That is true sainthood. That is true perfection in thy work. I shall leave this desert place where I have isolated myself from humankind, and I shall go down into the city slums and serve my fellow man. Then shall I be a saint, indeed, worthy of Thy fellowship!"

That is a parable which will be, and is, a comfort to all of us who have to labor in everyday ways and among everyday people. That is a parable for mothers who have to do the common chores of a home—washing dishes, sewing clothes, cooking meals. That is a parable for the father who works all day in a shop, store, or over books. That is a parable for the people—and they are myriad —who have to do the hard things of life for others.

Sainthood is doing what we do for people as though those people all had something of Christ in them—as though, through their personalities, they were sacred to him. That is true sainthood.

ଚ   ଓ

"IN THE SWEET BY AND BY"

In a village of about a thousand inhabitants, in Walworth County, Wisconsin, there was a country physician named Samuel Fillmore Bennett, who served several years in the Civil War as Lieutenant in the Fortieth Wisconsin Volunteers, who responded to Lincoln's first call.

He and J. P. Webster, a composer of music, were intimate friends. Webster was a person with a rather despondent nature, and he greatly depended upon the cheerful good humor and friendly optimism of his comrade. Perhaps that is why they were such intimate friends, because like attracted unlike then as it does now.

One day, in the late sixties, Webster, in a not too cheerful mood, went to see his friend Sam Bennett. It was in the after-

61

war depression period, and Webster felt that the end of all things good had come, that the world was going to the dogs, and that there wasn't much worth living for—a psychology that attacks many people in war and post-war days, always. Sam Bennett soon saw that his friend was in a particularly depressed mood that morning and said to him cheerfully and sympathetically, "What's the trouble now?"

"I'm completely discouraged, Sam. The war was bad enough, but this is worse. I can't see any hope ahead for any of us. We're shot to pieces financially, nationally, personally. The wounds of that awful war will never be healed. We'll never be a united and strong nation again; we'll never recover from the economic losses and much less from the national wounds of this war. The South will never forgive us."

And then his friend Sam Bennett replied: "It's all right, Webster. It will be all right by and by."

Like a flash, it occurred to Bennett that that was an eternal philosophy—something that not only he and his friend needed to learn, but something that the whole nation needed to learn. So he sat down at his desk and wrote with a pencil the words of the hymn "In the Sweet By and By."

Then the pessimistic Webster improvised the music on his old violin, jotting down the notes with a pencil. The words were written in half an hour, the music, by Webster in ten minutes, and in another ten minutes a group of friends in the village were singing it. One man in the group, R. R. Crosby, said to some friends standing by, "Gentlemen, that hymn will be one of the immortals."

✺   ✺

A LOOK AT THE STARS

A FEW years ago I had what the doctors called a nervous breakdown. It is a universal disease these days. Thousands of people have that trouble in one form or another, and I have found at least one cure for it.

In these days of rush and noise we are apt to get what we Americans have come to know as "The Jitters." We have another less dignified name for it, and that is "Ants in the Pants." It expresses itself in restlessness, irritability, lack of poise, anger, jealousy, and suspicion. In some cases it gets so bad that a strong man is afraid to cross a city street. One businessman I know used to hire a boy for ten cents to lead him across the street to his own office.

Two years ago, after ten years of ceaseless work in public speaking, teaching, writing, and radio, I was shot to pieces nervously and had to take a year off for a complete rest. I went to California.

But even rest, friends, and the California climate, did not seem to work much of a cure. Then, just by accident a friend invited me to go up to the top of Mount Hamilton one night to visit Lick Observatory. I was frightened by that long winding mountain road, which has in it 365 corkscrew turns, one for each day in the year. However, I went.

They allowed me to look through their high-powered Lick Observatory telescope that night. For the first time in my life I saw the stars in planes behind planes. With the human eye we see only stars in a single plane. But there I saw front yards full of stars, back yards, meadows and fields of stars, rivers of stars, forests of stars, long mountain ranges of stars—stars behind stars. I saw what astronomers now call the "Stellar Universe" which makes our solar system look like boys in a ring playing marbles. The friend who took me up there told the astronomer about my illness, and I saw that scientist's eyes sparkle as he said, "This is the best cure for nerves I know." That young astronomer pointed his telescope to a pin point in the universe and said to me: "Look at that, doctor. Look at that!" I looked.

Then he said: "That is Alpha Centauri, a star which is practically sitting on our back doorstep. It is only four light years

63

away. That means that its light which travels 186,000 miles a second takes four years to reach us."

Some time ago I saw a star burst. Actually it burst about the time of the Crusades, but the cosmic disaster was so far away that the news of it has just reached the earth. The light we saw then had taken all that time to get here.

When I came down from Mount Hamilton that evening I had several things to do that had before seemed important—letters to write, checks to send, plans to make. But now they all seemed picayune, trivial, unimportant. I was astonished that I had ever considered some of them important at all. For the moment I forgot my nerves and myself, lost in silent wonder and amazement at that universe I had seen from Lick Observatory.

Go look at the stars. It's a sure cure for the American jitters.

ↄ ○

HE LOST HIS HEAD COMPLETELY

A TOMBSTONE cutter was busily engaged in his shop when his friend dropped in for a visit. The friend, while looking about the shop, noticed a headstone which had been there for several years. The inscription had been cut on it, but the words were useless, for the stone had been in storage all that time. Curious, the friend asked why.

"The people who ordered it were not able to pay for it," came the laconic reply. "And it stays here till they bring the money."

"But what good is it doing you here?" the friend said.

"No good! No good at all!" replied the cutter with some anger.

"Well, then," continued his friend, "if those folks haven't been able to pay for it yet—it must be years—your chances of collecting are pretty slim. Did it ever occur to you that you might place that stone where it belongs? At least it will be doing some good. It just takes up valuable room here."

"That's poor business!" was the curt comment of the stone-cutter.

"It's never poor business to be kind to people and to go out of your way to help people who are in trouble." Having said this, the friend walked out of the shop and was on his way.

A month passed before he returned to that shop. He looked around the room. The stone was gone.

"Well, I see that you got rid of that stone," he commented. "Did they pay you for it?"

"No!" replied the stonecutter. "But I placed the stone where it belongs anyhow."

"That's poor business!" protested his friend, mockingly.

"I know it is," replied the stonecutter. "But after your last visit here my conscience started to torment me about it. I got to putting myself in that family's place, for I know that they haven't had the money to pay for it. Every time I came into this shop that white stone haunted me like a ghost until finally I took it out and put it where it really belongs. Then, afterwards, when I found out how happy it made the family, I lost my head completely."

"How?"

"Well, yesterday when they came in here to pay me for the stone, do you know what I did? I refused the money. That's how foolish I'm getting to be."

"Foolish? I wonder?" replied his friend.

ʊ   ʊ

HOW DO YOU DO, NEIGHBOR?

THIS is a story of what might be called a universal good neighbor policy, the story of a man named Hans, in Holland. Perhaps he had a last name but if so nobody remembers it. He was simply Hans of Holland to history.

He lived beside a blue canal surrounded by lovely green fields.

His home was a simple, low, peasant's hut with a windmill beside it, but the thing which characterized Hans was his neighborly spirit and his cheery greeting to everybody who passed him: "Good morning, neighbor. How do you do?"

After a while everybody waited for his cheery greeting. It was like a burst of sunshine on a gray day. It was like the coming of springtime.

One morning Hans walked past a stranger. The man was ragged and tired. He looked as if he hadn't eaten for a long time. Hans said to him: "Good morning, stranger. How do you do today?"

The stranger replied: "I do not do so well. I am ill and hungry, and those are the first kind words I have heard for many days. You see, my clothes look like the clothes of an outcast, and people shun me."

Hans took that ragged stranger into his little hut and gave him cheese and bread and milk. Then he put him to bed. The stranger slept soundly for the whole day and night through.

When he had risen the next morning he looked like a different man. There was a refined touch about him after a bath, and after he had donned one of Han's suits. When he had finished his breakfast, he said to Hans; "Now what can I do for you to repay this kindness?"

"I want nothing save to be kind to you and to see the change in your appearance and attitude," replied Hans. "That is pay enough for me, neighbor."

"I am a poor man. I can do little for you, but I can paint your picture," the stranger said. And he painted it that very morning.

The experience of being painted amused Hans. But months later he was more bewildered than amused when the king summoned him to Amsterdam to see the unveiling of that painting of himself standing beside a windmill.

A salvo of trumpets, and the king unveiled the painting—that immortal masterpiece. Then suddenly in the midst of the celebration a well-dressed man came up to Hans and said: "Good morning, neighbor. How are you today?" It was his beggar friend, one of Holland's master painters.

"But why am I here?" asked Hans.

"Oh, I told the king how you helped me—fed me, clothed me, gave me shelter, and then posed for me beside your cottage and windmill. You not only helped me, but you helped art also, for the painting is now prized throughout the continent. It has brought fame to our king and country. The king asked to see you, and here you are."

"Good morning, neighbor. How do you do?"

Yes, the good neighbor policy pays.

☙   ❧

A SPOT WHERE YOU CAN'T TURN BACK

RECENTLY an American pilot who ferries planes across the Atlantic said to a newspaper friend of mine when he was having dinner with him in between trips: "There's a spot in the Atlantic Ocean where you can't turn back."

"What do you mean by that?" my friend inquired.

"Well, it's this way: We start out in the early dawn or at midnight headed for England. We know how far we have come. We know how much gasoline we have used and what we have left and how much our motors are using. When we get to that spot I turn around and say to the kids, radio operator, and navigator, 'Well, this is the place. Shall we go on?'

"They always grin and yell back at me above the thunder of the engines: 'I'll say we'll go on! How are the motors?'

"I tell them that the motors are singing. Then those kids give me thumbs up. From that spot on there is no place to go but straight ahead through mist, darkness, cloud, or fog. And on we go!"

When I heard that story I was reminded once again of something Amelia Earhart said when she started over that same circle for the British Isles back in 1928. Amelia was about halfway across when an oil pipe started to leak, splashing her with oil and seriously endangering the airship. She had to make a quick decision whether to turn back or go ahead. As she hurtled onward, her motors missing, she said to herself, "The perils of turning back are greater than the perils of going ahead, so I'll go on."

That is exactly what she did, and she was the first woman to fly the Atlantic alone.

ᵓ ᵓ

HOW TO PRAY WITHOUT CEASING

ONE of my friends recently sent me a homely and a homey story which I like and want to pass on to my readers.

She says that a number of ministers were gathered together discussing how the command to "pray without ceasing" could be complied with. One of the number was appointed to write a paper on that theme and present it to the next meeting.

The maid who was working in that home overheard the discussion, and she said to the minister: "What? Waiting a whole month until the next meeting to find out the meaning of the simplest text in the Bible? Why, I can give you the answer to that."

"Well, Mary, replied the minister, "can you tell me how to 'pray without ceasing'? How do you understand it? Can you pray all the time when you have so many things to do?"

"Why, yes sir," said Mary. "The more things I have to do, the more I can pray."

"Tell me how you do it," replied the minister.

"Well," the girl said: "when I open my eyes in the morning I pray: 'Lord, open my eyes to understanding.' Then when I am dressing I pray that I may be clothed with the garments of

68

righteousness. When I am washing myself I ask God for the washing of my soul and thought. When I begin my daily work I pray that I have what the Bible promised—'strength for the day.' When I kindle the fire I pray that God may set the fire of righteousness burning in my heart. When I begin to sweep out the house I pray that my own heart may be cleansed of all impurities, dirt, and bad thinking. When I am preparing and partaking of breakfast I ask God that he will give me my daily bread and that I may be fed with the manna and the 'sincere milk' of his word.

"When I am busy with taking care of little children I look to God as my Father and pray to the Christ, who took little children into his arms and blessed them and said, 'of such is the kingdom of heaven.' When I have worked all day and go out into the starlight to gather in the clothes which have been hanging on the line—like they have been today—I look up at the hills and stars and say to myself: 'I will lift up mine eyes unto the hills from whence cometh my help and unto the stars.' I may mix up the scriptures a little, but at least I know them well enough to pray without ceasing."

"Enough!" cried the preacher. "These things are revealed unto babes and often hid from the wise and the prudent. Go on, Mary, you certainly know more about how to pray without ceasing than we ministers do."

It is a simple story out of everyday life, and it needs no amplification or application from me. All I know is, that if we followed that practice we would get more out of life than most of us do, and that includes preachers and priests.

ᘓ   ᘖ

FALLING ON THE BALL

BRANCH RICKEY, famous in contemporary life as manager of the St. Louis Cardinals ball team, and later of the Brooklyn Dodgers, has a chapter in his life which few sportsmen know. He was a football coach for several years, and I played fullback on one of his teams at Allegheny College back in the early part of this century. Branch was as good a football coach as he has been ball player and manager of successful World-Series-winning ball teams.

Branch Rickey taught me one of the most important lessons I ever learned.

I had an exalted idea of my importance to the Allegheny College team. I felt that it was beneath my dignity as one of the "Stars" of the team who could run a hundred yards in ten seconds and who could shoot a forward pass with speed and accuracy to demean myself in practice periods by "falling on the ball." Besides, I skinned my elbows, hands, and legs falling on the frozen ground.

"Falling on the ball" seemed child's play to me. I couldn't see much sense in an old veteran senior player having to do what all the scrubs did. "Falling on the ball' was to me the ABC's of football.

But one day Branch Rickey took me aside and talked to me like a Dutch Uncle. He told me that no man could be a real player who wasn't willing to practice on the basic fundamentals of football; who hadn't learned to fall on the ball when it was fumbled; to do it unconsciously, with relaxed and limbered limbs until he couldn't injure himself even if he tried; that the man who was always trying to save himself was the one who, invariably, got hurt; that the man who hurled his body in complete abandonment and self-forgetfulness on the fumbled ball, whenever and wherever it fell, was the player who came out unscratched; but that the man who fell carefully, gingerly, and who tried to protect himself, was the one who always got hurt.

Said Rickey: "Think of saving yourself and you will get hurt, sure! Forget yourself and you will be doing your duty, pick up that fumble for your team, maybe make a touchdown and win the game."

Then he added this sentence like the crack of a whip: "And—

if you don't want to practice falling on the ball like the poorest scrub on this team—hand in your uniform. We need you, but we don't need you that much!"

Branch Rickey was right. We have a lot of falling on the ball to do in life. We have to learn Latin verbs, multiplication tables; we have to wash dishes, scrub floors, darn little stockings. Fathers have to work in mills and do the menial chores of life in order to keep the home intact; in order to keep the nation moving toward its destined goals.

Every phase of life has its drudgery, its "falling on the ball," but often the man who is willing to perfect the art of "falling on the ball" wins the big games of life, or helps to win them. Such men as Doctors Banting, Best, Mayo—they all have to do a lot of the drudgery of life; they have to learn to fall on the ball. Life is like that in all of its phases.

ʊ ʊ

"I KNEW YOU'D COME THROUGH, MOTHER!"

A FRIEND of mine told me a glorious story the other evening. Her daughter was to have her first-born child in a distant city, and the mother pawned her wedding ring and took a train to be with her in this first experience of young motherhood.

As the mother sat by her daughter's side during the travail, the daughter kept saying to her: "Hold on to my hand, Mother. It will be easier to bear if I can just have the feel of your hand in mine!"

The mother held on, the child was born; but following the baby's birth it became necessary for the young mother to have a blood transfusion.

Several nurses and friends were tested, but the mother was the only one who had the right blood count, so she gave the transfusion. She did it willingly and as a matter of course, never thinking of herself as heroic.

71

However, an hour later when she went into the room where her daughter was lying and saw the color returning to her pale cheeks, the new life and animation in her eyes—all the result of the transfusion she had just given her—the mother was overcome with emotion, felt herself getting faint, started for the door, but dropped on the floor before she could reach it. The daughter was frightened, for she suddenly realized that it was her own mother who had given the blood.

After the excitement had died down, and the mother and daughter were alone, the daughter said: "Mother, I have always known from childhood that when I needed you you would be right there on the job. Whenever I have been troubled you have always come. I have learned to count on that as one of the universal laws of life. And Oh, boy, you certainly came through this time! You always do!"

When the mother told me this story she added: "That was worth all the sacrifices I ever made for my daughter. When she said in her girlish slang: 'I knew you'd come through, Mother! You always do!' that was the most thrilling commendation I ever received.

ꙅ   ꙅ

SECRET SPLENDOR

I LIVE between two Jewish neighbors. One of them has a beautiful lawn of grass that always looks green and shimmering no matter how little rain has fallen on it because he knows how to take care of a lawn. He also has fine flowers and frequently presents me with cuttings from rare plants.

He says to me, and I believe him, "Your seeds will blow over into my garden, friend, and if you don't have good plants I won't have either; so we must both keep our yards fine if the other is to have a fine yard."

I have been going to school to my Jewish neighbor for years.

On the other side of me another Jewish neighbor has two fine children. I like them and they like me. Those children, a boy and a girl, are both under five. We are pals. One day one of the children said to me: "My daddy told my mother last night that you're nice and that he likes you."

I went into my home with little songs singing in my heart at that child's good news, and from that minute on I had a warm feeling toward my Jewish neighbor on the other side of me.

In our village there is a Jewish druggist I like. He is round and fat and friendly, and when I go into his store I feel that he is glad to see me. In fact, he makes me feel so much as if mere business is a personal matter that I pass ten drug stores to get to his store every day of my life. One day I said to him: "Mr. Dorenbaum, I don't want to buy a thing today. I tried to think up an excuse to come in here just to talk with you. I like to come into your store."

He smiled and replied: "That's the way I feel about your coming in, doctor. It's good to see you every day. It makes my day better." Then he added thoughtfully: "Friends are better than money any day with me."

All the way home that sentence kept ringing in my heart. That man is right, for there is what Edwin Markham always called "A Secret Splendor" about friendship.

In fact, Markham put it all into a little verse like this:

> Shine on me, Secret Splendor, till I feel
> That all are one upon the mighty wheel.
> Let me be brother to the meanest clod,
> Knowing he, too, bears on the dream of God;
> Yet be fastidious, and have such friends
> That when I think of them my soul ascends!

ꙅ   ꙅ

"UNSPOILED AND UNAFRAID"

SERGEANT YORK, one of the unforgotten heroes of the last war, has come to his own after twenty-three years of comparative obscurity in his Tennessee hills, founding and running a school for mountain boys and girls. With the glare of publicity thrown on him following his World War exploits, many wondered what sort of a man he was to turn down offers of wealth and fame to go back into the hills from whence he came to serve his fellow beings. But it is still true that you cannot hide a light under a bushel, and that the world will make a beaten path to your door if you can build a better mousetrap.

If these sayings had never been proved true before, they have been recently in the life of this simple, humble, converted Christian churchman; for what is said to be the finest motion picture ever made has been made about him. The President of the United States quoted him in his 1941 Armistice Day speech at Arlington National Cemetery; and John G. Winant, United States Ambassador to Great Britain, also quoted Sergeant York in Edinburgh, Scotland, when receiving the honorary degree of Doctor of Laws.

Mr. Winant, in his journey through Edinburgh, visited the American-Scottish Memorial in Princess Street. Referring to that Memorial, Mr. Winant said that the statue had a strange likeness to Sergeant York, whom General Pershing commended as the bravest soldier in the American Expeditionary Force. Then Mr. Winant said, "York still lives, a simple citizen of the Tennessee mountains, unspoiled and unafraid."

❧   ☙

"AS EMPTY AS A LAST YEAR'S NEST"

THE summer is over, the fall leaves begin to drift slowly to the ground, crimson and golden tapestries are spread on every hill.

The sumac and maple have sent forth their crimson flames; "The frost is on the pumpkin"; and Riley's "fodder's in the shock."

Our sons and daughters are off to college, and the house has an empty ring. Their gay laughter and their loud repartee leave the rooms of a home hollow like some great cave. The best phrase to describe the feeling we all have when they have gone off to college is one which Bishop William A. Quayle used once when he said, "Our rooms are as empty as a last year's nest."

So they are, and I have tried to put that feeling into a few lines of verse: I wrote these lines one fall not long ago when my own daughter went off to Smith College and left our home empty and desolate. I remember vividly the evening she went away to college. I had that same feeling more intensified the evening I married her to a fine young chap and he took her away to his own home. I walked back into her room and fingered over every little thing she had left behind. I looked at her dresser, her closet, and her bed. They were all "as empty as a last year's nest." That is the only phrase which describes that room.

Then I walked out into our yard and looked up into a tree, where all summer long we had had a Baltimore oriole's nest. We had watched the mother oriole build that nest. We watched the young birds teeter on the edge of that nest and learn to fly under her careful tutelage. We watched them darting about all summer in their golden and orange colorings, flashing through the sunlight. Then we saw them all take their own youthful way. That is as it should be. Both of us knew that in our own daughter's case, but it was a wrench both when she went off to college and when she went off to a home of her own.

The fall she went off to college I went out and looked at that empty oriole's nest hanging in the tree and then went back and wrote a little verse which I called "As Empty as a Last Year's Nest." The last verse of it reads:

> There are so many empty rooms
> These autumn days of gold,

75

> Where memories of summer days
> Like leaves of love unfold.
> Since they went off to college,
> Upon an ancient quest,
> Their rooms are lone and empty
> As a last year's nest.

Why did I write this piece? Oh, just to let other fathers and mothers who have sent their children off to college and to homes of their own know that we too have walked where they have walked.

❧ ❦

"AND NO LIE WILL SERVE!"

Some time ago I read a news dispatch which was headed "Slayer's Greatest Fear Is That He Won't Be Executed," and then followed one of those unusually dramatic news stories of one Eldon Hawks, who was condemned to die in California for murder.

The psychiatrists said of him: "He has been in such a state for weeks and is eager for the transition from one life to another."

The Episcopal chaplain who attended him explained it this way: "Hawks wants to die because he has a definite feeling that the life to come is to be beautiful. He doesn't want to miss that. He's not going to spend the rest of his normal life in prison when he feels he can get something better by dying."

Hawks himself, when his victim's widow asked Governor Olsen to pardon him, wrote to the executive, saying: "I have feared you may be foolish enough to listen to her nonsense. You have no legitimate grounds on which to commute me. I murdered a man in cold blood. I deserve my penalty. I planned the murder and if I was out tomorrow I would go on with my criminal life."

Strange story. Strange attitude. And it brings to my memory a dramatic scene from *Barabbas,* Marie Corelli's great novel on

76

that same theme, and with a challenging philosophy which Hawks' life does not seem to get:

"Knowest thou, excellent Barabbas, what is this death?"

"All men know what it is," replied Barabbas drearily: "A choking of the breath, a blindness of the eyes, a darkness, silence, and an end!"

"Nay, not an end but a beginning!" said Melchior, rising and confronting him, his eyes flashing with enthusiasm. "That choking of the breath, that blindness of the eyes; those are the throes of birth, not death! Even as the new-born child struggles for air and cannot too suddenly endure the full unshaded light of day, so does the new-born soul, that struggles forth from out its fleshly womb, fight gaspingly for strength to take its first deep breathing in of living glory. 'A darkness and a silence,' sayest thou? Not so! a radiance and a music! a wondrous clamour of the angels' voices ringing out melodies aloft like harps in tune! And of the spirit lately parted from the earth, they ask: 'What bringest thou? What message does thou bear? Hast thou made the sad world happier, wiser, fairer?' And over all the deathless voice of marvel thunders: 'Soul of a man! What hast thou done?' And that great question must be met and answered; and no lie will serve!"

It is well to ponder those fine lines and to be ready, when we make the great transition to that other land of living, to give an accounting of something fine we have done; for "no lie will serve!"

ᘐ   ᘐ

"DON'T LET THE CANDLE GO OUT!"

A SIX-YEAR-OLD was sitting on his father's lap on Christmas night looking at his Christmas tree. He had been permitted to stay up until the unheard-of hour of nine as a special concession.

Suddenly he dropped off to sleep and dreamed a dream. He dreamed that an angel came down from heaven. Starting at the top of the beautiful Christmas tree the angel snuffed out every candle on it but one—the one at the top. That candle the angel carried over to the little boy. Handing it to him, she said: "Here is the candle of Christmas light and love. Never let it go out!"

The little boy stirred uneasily in his daddy's lap as he dreamed, and muttered aloud something about candles, trees, and an angel.

The father took the little fellow up to bed and tucked him in. Just before he turned to go he bent over and kissed the boy good night. Then as he lifted himself from the bed the boy aroused, put his arms around his daddy, hugged him close, and said, "Don't let the angel go away, Daddy. And don't let the candle go out!"

In that child's Christmas dream lies all the hope of the world. "How far that little candle throws his beams!" If we could keep the Christmas spirit of light and love alive this would be a kindlier world.

There is more to that story than a child's dream. "Don't let the angel go away. And don't let the candle go out!"

ව   උ

"AN HOUR OF GLORY"

I USED to visit a dear old woman who was in her nineties. Her body was feeble, but her spirit was valiant.

I never knew a more cheerful person, and frequently I allowed her to think I was calling on her for her sake, when all the time I was doing it for my own sake. I used to go there when I was out of ideas, or blue and disheartened. I went to get new ideas from her and to have her take me under the spiritual armpits and lift me up again until I walked with God among the stars. And she invariably did it.

On one such visit I said to her: "Mrs. Sansom, just what is the heart of your power and poise? Just what is it that keeps you so happy, contented, and cheerful when you have to sit here all alone most of the day?"

She smiled and said, "I had an hour of glory upon a wind-swept hill!"

I was thrilled by that sentence. She saw it and added:

I read that line this very morning in a poem by Grace Noll Crowell. The poet told in that poem of how she looked back on what she called "old remembered days," and how some hours in her life stood out "like silver in the sun." She told in that poem of certain snow-swept days when she had to remain alone in her invalid room. She got out some books of poems which she loved, she got out some old albums with pictures of the past in them. She got out a scrapbook full of ancient and beautiful memories; memories of "green gold" days in June; memories of a lover's proposal; memories of a father's farewell at a railroad station at early dawn; memories of childhood in the old hay loft; memories of school days and friends. She relived those incidents when she read them in her scrapbook. And they were just as real to her as the day they happened.

Then that wise poet concluded her poem by tying up memories of the past with memory-making for today when she said:

Yet as I lived them, strange I did not know
Which hours were destined thus to live and shine,
And which among the countless ones would grow
To be, peculiarly, forever mine.
If I but wait, perhaps, this hour will be
Like silver in the sun, some day, to me!

That's the secret of it, my friend. I sit here and go back over my hours of glory. Everybody has them. I have had many of them. I am still having them. That's what makes life livable for me. Now, go on about your business and be happy, looking for your "hour of glory upon a windswept hill."

ॐ ॐ

FULL MEASURE AND OVERFLOWING

OUT near Concord, Massachusetts, there is a wayside vegetable stand which we like to patronize.

The reason we drive ten miles out of our way to patronize that stand is because of an experience we had there years ago. That day we were total strangers to the Italian family which runs that stand.

I ordered a peck of peaches, and when the fine, tanned, tall, rugged Italian boy who waited on me had filled the peck to overflowing so that the peaces ran off the top and fell to the ground, I said: "Hey there, pal, you are giving more than good measure!"

"Oh, we always like to give good measure, full and overflowing," he replied. Then he added with a wink: "It's good business!"

After he had emptied that peck into a paper sack he added a few additional peaches.

"But what do you get out of that kind of business?" I asked him, with an assumed cynicism which I really did not feel inside of me. "You'll go bankrupt doing that!"

"We been here five years, and we haven't gone bankrupt yet doing that. Father says that being generous doesn't hurt our business any. Besides, there's something to business besides making money, and you know that."

There was a slight rebuke in that Italian boy's last phrase. Perhaps he assumed by the look of me that I ought to know that. If he did, it was a compliment which I did not hope for.

But that boy was right, for we have been going to that stand now for more than ten years and you couldn't drag us away from them. In fact, we pass fifty roadside stands to reach that one, and even in days of gas conservation and rationing, we still use up that additional gas to go there when we could get our fruit and vegetables much nearer home.

That Italian boy has a standard of measurement which wins friends for him. First of all, his stuff is always good. That never fails. Second, he always has a smile and soon gets to know his customers by name. Third, he believes in giving full measure, heaped and running over. So we have told all of our friends about him, and at least fifty of them patronize that stand all the time.

80

In the years that we have been going there, two of the boys have grown to manhood; one has gone through Tuft's College, another has married and has two children. We have been as interested in their personal affairs as if they were our own children. I never think of them that I do not remember a biblical phrase, "With what measure ye mete, it shall be measured to you." They have learned to get the most out of life by giving the most to life.

❦   ❧

FLOWERS GROW IN CANYONS OF SORROW

ONE day several years ago Ralph Connor, the famous Canadian novelist, was visiting in my home. My daughter Betty had just broken her leg in the high school gymnasium, and she thought the end of the world had come. She was missing at least two dances, half a dozen parties, and football games galore. It was a supreme tragedy. She was complaining to Ralph Connor about it all as he sat in her room. That great and gracious man smiled and then told her this parable:

In my book *The Sky Pilot* I tell a story about a little girl near your age. Her name was Gwen, and she was a wild, willful lassie who always wanted her own way. One day while riding her horse she met with a terrible accident, and she was a cripple for life. She became very rebellious, and "The Sky Pilot," the missionary preacher, came to visit her. When he saw her rebellion he told her the following story:

"For many centuries in this country there were no canyons but only the broad, wide prairies. One day the master of the prairie, walking over these great plains where there grew only brown grass, said to the prairie: 'Where are your flowers?' And the prairie answered: 'Master, I have no seeds.' Then the master of the prairie said to the birds, 'Bring seeds for the prairie, my birds!'

"And the birds carried seeds of every kind of flower and scattered them over all the prairie. Soon the prairie bloomed with crocuses,

81

roses, buffalo beans, and the yellow crowfoot. Later came wild sun-flowers and red lilies.

"The master came and was well pleased. But he missed the flowers he loved most of all and said to the prairie: 'But where are the clematis and columbines, sweet violets, windflowers, and all the ferns and flowering shrubs?'

"Again he spoke to the birds, and again they scattered seeds far and wide. But when the master came again he could not find the flowers he loved most of all and said: 'But where are my sweetest flowers?' And the prairie replied sorrowfully: 'Oh, master, I cannot keep those particular flowers, for the winds blow fiercely, and the sun beats down upon my breast, and they are blown away.'

"Then the Master spoke to the lightning, the thunder and clouds and down came a torrent, a hurricane, a flood which washed out deep gullies. After that storm and upheaval, once again the birds carried the seeds the master loved most of all: clematis, columbine, sweet violets and windflowers. This time they grew safely for they were sheltered by the deep canyons and gullies. They needed shelter to grow."

Then the Sky Pilot said to the little crippled Gwen: "These are the spiritual canyon flowers: gentleness, meekness, long-suffering. They bloom in the deep cuts of life."

"But there are no flowers blooming in my canyon of suffering," said Gwen wistfully.

"Some day they will bloom, Gwen. The master will find them, and we too shall see them."

Betty smiled as Ralph Connor told her that story. It needed no moralizing. In the canyon of her temporary suffering the flowers were already beginning to bloom.

☙   ❦

A SINGLE DAY OF ETERNITY

OF all the books, articles, and radio talks that I have read and heard from Hendrik Van Loon there is one simple paragraph which stands out in my memory like the silhouette of a lonely tree against a crimson sunset at evening. That single sentence is under the first illustration in his book *The Story of Mankind.*

High up in the North in the land called Svithjod, there stands a rock. It is a hundred miles high and a hundred miles wide. Once every thousand years a little bird comes to this rock to sharpen its beak.

When the rock has thus been worn away, then a single day of eternity will have gone by.

I wonder if Winston Churchill didn't have that mood in his heart—a sense of God's eternity—when he said these words over the radio, following the immortal Atlantic meeting with President Roosevelt:

We had a service on Sunday in our Atlantic Bay. The President came on the quarter-deck of the "Prince of Wales" where there were mingled together many hundreds of American and British sailors and marines. The sun shone bright and warm while we all sang old hymns which are our common inheritance and which John Hampden's soldiers sang when they bore his body to the grave, and in which the brief, precarious span of human life is contrasted with one to whom a thousand ages are but as yesterday when it is past, as a watch in the night.

The hymn to which he referred is "O God, Our Help in Ages Past," and it was written by Isaac Watts. It is a rendering of the ninetieth Psalm. It was written about 1714, shortly before the death of Queen Anne, during the time of anxiety in England as to the identity of her successor. Thackeray referred to this great hymn in the closing chapters of *Henry Esmond.* F. J. Gilman called it "the great ceremonial hymn of the English nations." Winston Churchill's reference to it in his radio address to the English-speaking peoples is but another accolade for its popularity, its helpfulness, and its universal appropriateness. The particular line to which Churchill referred reads:

> A thousand ages, in thy sight,
> Are like an evening gone;

> Short as the watch that ends the night,
> Before the rising sun.

It is undoubtedly one of the two or three most popular and helpful hymns of the English-speaking churches and has been translated into every language and dialect on the earth, for it gives to human beings who sing it a sense of the eternal in times of need.

❂　　❂

FORGET IT NOT

I ONCE stood with Edwin Markham on the shores of the North Maine Ocean, near Christmas Cove.

As far as we could see, jutting black rocks loomed before us—no sand, no grass, no trees—just jutting black, aged rocks, with here and there on the bare rocks a patch of moss, lichen, or a stray bit of seaweed. But always the beat of the restless waves and always the splash of the green spray above the waves, which were unceasingly pounding those rocks.

"What do you think of this beautiful scene?" Mr. Markham asked the native Maine fisherman who stood with us.

"It's beautiful," replied the native.

"But doesn't it get monotonous after a while? After all, it's always the same—the rocks, the sea, and the sky."

"Not at all!" replied the fisherman. "Because there is more here than just that. There is mystery, infinity. Take the sea, for instance, the endlessly rolling sea. Yesterday we saw the rise and fall of the tide. We see it today. And I know that each tomorrow will look upon the same faithful tides and waves. Why, this sea was my earliest hero and my first memory. I have learned to admire the tenacity, the ceaselessness of the roll of the sea, and the breaking of the waves on these rocks."

Mr. Markham nodded his approval and understanding of what this native was saying. Then the fisherman went on:

"And that ocean out there. It's the same ocean that followed the voyage of Magellan, Columbus, and our pioneer Pilgrim ancestors. Perhaps some drop of water we see today licked the hot shores of India or Panama. Uninteresting? I should say not, Mr. Poet. It's too full of history and romance to be uninteresting!"

Mr. Markham nodded an understanding head again, and the Maine native went on: "But my real heroes are these rocks. See how strong they are and how fearless. No matter how mightily the waves pound them, those rocks stand firm! I used to favor the sea. It was my first love. But now I favor these rocks. Water can all evaporate, but these rocks still stand forever!"

We stood silently for a few minutes and then, like the voice of a ghost in the mist, the poet, with his white hair flying in the winds, for all the world like the white mists, said: "But the rocks, too, will crumble away in time. However, there is something that will stand for all time."

"And what is that, Mr. Poet?" the fisherman asked.

"Love!" replied Mr. Markham. "I have written some lines about it:

> Forget it not till the crowns are crumbled
>   And the swords of the Kings are rent with rust—
> Forget it not till the hills lie humbled,
>   And the springs of the seas run dust.

☙   ❧

THE ONLY WAY OUT IS UP

I WAS talking with a friend the other day, and he told me a good story. He was lying in a hospital with a broken leg, and I was calling on him. He was utterly discouraged, disgusted, restless. He had to lie there for three weeks as the result of a bad fracture.

The nurse had gone out of the room, and he had no visitors, so he was doubly discouraged. In addition to that it was a gray November day with intermittent rain and little sunshine. All he could see out of his window was a gray brick wall, flat and uninviting. However, in the midst of that gray day suddenly the sun shone on a Virginia creeper which had climbed from the ground forty feet below until it reached almost to the top of that four-story hospital wall. Each leaf of that creeper was tipped with crimson. Its crimson beauty spread itself over the buff brick wall like a blanket of crimson. It was a glorious sight, and it heartened my friend no end.

But another thing heartened him even more. As he lay there he thought of all the years it had taken the creeper to struggle up to that four-story height. It had, as he estimated it, taken at least twenty years. Fraction of an inch by fraction of an inch, brick by brick, it had struggled upward. The soil down in the dark courtyard was not any too rich. It had little care taken of it, but up and up and up it had struggled through the years. It had literally come up out of a well, for the courtyard was a deep dark pit. As my friend lay there it suddenly occurred to him that the only way out for that vine was up, and as that thought occurred to him he almost leapt out of his bed. That was true for him as well as for that vine. The only way out of the well of loneliness into which he had fallen through no fault of our own was up. The only way out was up and on.

I have a farmer friend who fell into an old well about a year ago. The well was thirty feet deep, slippery and steep. When he realized what a dangerous spot he was in, he was at first paralyzed with fear. He yelled for an hour. Then he began to get chilly and numb. For the first time since he had fallen into that well he looked above him and saw a circle of light. Above that light was shining a star. That was the first time he had ever seen a star in the day time, but the depth and the darkness of the well made it possible to see that star. He told me that when he saw the circle of light and the star he said to himself: "Well, there is only one way to go, and that is toward that star and

86

circle of light. That means up!" So laboriously, for five hours, he dug steps in the soft wall of the slanting well and climbed to safety.

So it is with all of us. The only way out of any mess we get into is up and on.

ↄ   ☾

THE SHADOW OF A MAN

A GROUP of men sat in a smoke-filled club room. They were young men and after discussing politics, women, and war, they finally fell into more serious themes of conversation, each of them telling what he would most like to do and be in the life that was ahead.

Finally a tall, sunburned, distinctly good looking lad bluntly gave his testimony by saying: "I want to be a millionaire."

The others smiled; some laughed out loud.

"Who doesn't?" asked one young blond.

"No! I mean it!" the tall and dark boy responded. "No, not for what the money could do for me. Not that at all. But imagine what good a rich man could do if he so desired. I've seen some of the desperate poverty of the slums, and I have felt just as young King Edward did when he said, 'Something's got to be done about this!' I think of friends I could help, members of my own family, a young sister who is married and paying for a home. I want to help her get some of the things she wants. I know people who, if they had a little help right now, could change their whole lives."

The crowd was silenced by the boy's apparent sincerity, and one friend said: "I can add nothing to that wish of yours, but I can think of something even more thrilling, and that is to give without others knowing about it; and something even more thrilling than that—to give without even knowing it yourself. Like the old legend that my mother used to tell me when I was a child."

"What was that?" the whole crowd yelled.

Then the speaker told this story:

There is a legend of a saint whose wonderful deeds astonished the world. Even the angels in heaven were astonished until they learned the secret of this good saint. Everywhere that man went he diffused virtue, as a flower gives out perfume, without even being aware of it himself. He left an aroma of love and kindness behind him wherever he went. The angels one day asked that he be given the gift of miracles, and God consented. They asked the man if he would like the touch of his hand to heal the sick.

"No," he replied, "I would rather God should do that."

"Then would you like to convert guilty souls and bring them back to right living?"

"No," replied the saint. "It is the Spirit's mission to do that. I only pray!"

"Would you like to be a model of patience and draw men by your piety?"

"No! If men were attracted to me they might be estranged from God."

"What do you desire?" asked the angels.

"That God would give me the gift of doing a good deal of good without knowing it even myself" he replied simply and sincerely.

The angels were perplexed, but finally they resolved that wherever the shadow of that saint should fall it should cure disease and comfort all sorrow. So it came to pass that, as the saint passed along the earth the hearts of men were cheered. And wherever his shadow fell tears were wiped away, sunshine swept from behind clouds, little children laughed, and tired men were rested."

And the group of young businessmen in the smoke-filled club room agreed that was the greatest gift of all—to do good without even knowing it yourself, to do good instinctively, unconsciously, automatically.

ↄ　ɔ

GAMBLING ON GOD

LAST summer I visited Plymouth, the landing place of our Pilgrim Fathers. On a hill above that historic city there is a monument to the Pilgrims. On a high granite pedestal there is a colossal figure of Liberty. That figure stands looking back across the sea over which our Pilgrim ancestors sailed so long ago, seeking for a freedom which they did not have in Europe. One hand of that figure is raised aloft with a finger pointing into the skies, symbolic of the fact that they were God-guided in their voyage to this new land and this free land. They had gambled on God, and they had won—for themselves and for more than one hundred and thirty million people who live in that land today.

As I stood there I not only thought of them, but I also thought of that other gambler, Christopher Columbus, who had also, long before them, dared unknown seas. He, as they, had "gone but joyously launching his ships fearlessly into the dark unknown," because he believed in something, and he dared to gamble his life, his future, his reputation on his belief and his dream. One great historian said of Columbus:

"The belief that the East could be reached by sailing westward was held by many learned men, and was not original with Columbus; but he was the first and only man of his time who was ready to gamble on that belief and risk his all in an attempt to demonstrate the theory. For this he deserves a place among the greatest characters of history."

History also adds: "He reached the conclusion, which became the settled conviction of his mind, not only that the East could be reached by sailing west, but also that God had raised him to accomplish this great work for mankind, and from this conviction he never wavered to the last day of his life."

It was because of this spirit that Edwin Markham says of Columbus in his poem:

> He knew he was (his constant boast)
> A servant of the Holy Ghost.

Then continues the historian: "His greatness consisted, not in his conception of a new thought, for the thought was old, nor for doing for the world a thing that no other man could have done, but in his willingness to undertake and to demonstrate the truth of his theory. He dared to do where others only talked and theorized. In this he stood far above every other man of his time."

It was because of this spirit that Markham has Columbus say to his men on that voyage:

> Set sail, my men, the hour has come,
> For shipwreck or Millennium!

In that mood Columbus was willing to gamble on his knowledge, his vision, his dream, his faith, his life. He was willing to take a chance on shipwreck or millennium. He was willing to gamble on God!

ᴅ   ᴄ

THE SOUTHERN CROSS OVER JAVA

SEVERAL years ago I was sailing out of Singapore on the Dutch steamer "Markus," headed for Batavia, in Java. As our little steamer sailed through that Singapore Harbor I looked back. A cool tropical wind was blowing that evening, but back of us was a splashing, tumultuous, tumbling tropical sunset flaming across the sky. In the direct path of that flaring sun a lighthouse flashed its blinking eyes like a musical director with his baton beating time to the rhythm of the wind and the tumult of that orchestral sunset. Then, suddenly, night fell, and an ominous feeling was in the air as that little ship plunged southward toward Java. About midnight we were in the very vortex of as terrific a typhoon as I ever lived through.

I was tossed out of my berth. Dressing hurriedly with a good deal of fear, I went to the bridge of that little steamer to be with the captain whom I knew rather intimately.

In less than an hour we were being tossed about as if we were a rowboat. I was terrified, and I watched the captain's face. He tried to smile, but there wasn't much heart in it. He could not speak English, and I could not speak Dutch although I knew him well. For four hours we stood on that bridge, and both of us had to cling to the railing to keep from being thrown down.

After four hours of this tropical typhoon I was nearly exhausted physically. I had long since given up spiritually and was resigned to sinking. Then I saw a light in that Dutch captain's eyes as he pointed with his hand to the south toward Java. It took me five minutes to see what he meant, but finally I could make out a single star high in the sky to the south. That was the first light we had seen since the flashing of the lighthouse the evening before as we left Singapore Harbor, and it cheered my heart and filled me with hope in spite of the fact that that little Dutch ship was still plunging until its bow seemed to stand up straight in the air.

But the Dutch captain seemed to be trying to point out something more than that single star. However, I couldn't understand his signs. Then the clouds parted a bit wider, and I saw two more stars, one to the east and the other to the west. Three stars that seemed to form a triangle in the southern sky. I drew a triangle on a piece of paper to indicate that I understood. But he shook his head and took the pencil and drew a cross beside my triangle. Then with almost hysterical joy and elation he again pointed into the southern skies toward Java; and there it was!

The storm had blown the clouds back like a great curtain and there, in all of its glory, was my first glimpse of the constellation they call "The Southern Cross." My upbringing had been so steeped in Christian tradition that when I looked at the Southern Cross, shining there over Java, I felt a sense of peace; and all fear left me, although the storm was still tossing us about as if we were a canoe on the sea.

ᘖ   ᘗ

THE WAY OF THE GREAT

The first distinguished man I ever interviewed was Luther Burbank. I was a young minister in San Jose, California. Burbank had just created his Burbank potato; had just bred the thorns and poison out of the desert Cactus and made it edible for horses and cattle; had just created the famous Shasta daisy; and was called "The Plant Wizard"—a name, by the way, which he disliked a great deal.

I was young and didn't know that I ought to write a letter to such a great and busy man before attempting to see him, so I climbed into my first car and drove from San Jose to Santa Rosa without even the slight formality of telling him that I was coming. I now realize that was a good illustration of the old phrase "Fools rush in where angels fear to tread."

I arrived one morning about eleven o'clock and nonchalantly knocked at the door.

A bright, black-haired young lady asked what I wanted. I said: "I want to see Mr. Burbank."

"Have you an engagement?"

I did not have and told her so.

"Well, I'm sorry, but you can't see Mr. Burbank. Hundreds of people come here every week to see him—come from all over the world. All of his time would be taken up in interviews if we did not have some limitations. You should have written a letter before coming."

I stammered a bit, told her that I was a young preacher, that I had read so much about him, that I wanted to talk about his plant experiments, that . . .

I was about to tell that formidable person, whom I didn't even know, that I should have written a letter before coming, when suddenly there glided into that room a little gray-haired man with a smile on his face. He turned to the secretary, who barred me from the door, and said graciously:

"My goodness, Miss Mary, didn't I tell you about the letter I got from Mr. Stidger? That was careless of me. And I sent him a post card telling him to come this morning. Forgive me. Come in, Mr. Stidger. I'm always glad to talk with a minister, for we are all in this same business—trying to fathom God's secrets. Come right in."

The young lady had a wicked look in her eyes but smiled as she let me in. I think she must have forgiven Luther Burbank for that little white and kindly fib, for she later married him. But whether she did or not, his action on that morning gave me a look into the life of a truly great and thoughtful man, and also a hospitable man, for he kept me for lunch, dinner, and the night. And in between times he took me about his experimental gardens at Santa Rosa and Sebastapol and told me of his exciting experiments.

The great, I then learned, do not live by the letter of the law but are laws unto themselves. Also I learned on that wonderful visit how generous and kindly and adaptable the truly great can be.

ↄ   ヮ

THREE GATES OF GOLD

YEARS ago while I was traveling in China those quaint people told me an interesting tale of what they called "Three Gates of God."

The legend admonishes those who are tempted to pass on a bit of unkind gossip or scandal to test that intruding "Witch of Gossip" by making her pass through the first gate of gold. That gate is called the "Is It True?" gate.

If most of us would compel the "Witch of Gossip" to pass through this testing gate of gold, most of the things that she tells us we would never repeat to others. In fact, we wouldn't even listen to them ourselves. Even that first test would eliminate most of the gossip that runs rampant among us.

The second gate of gold is the gate the Chinese call "Is It

Needful?" If even that simple question were asked of this old "Witch of Gossip" 90 percent of the harmful talk in small towns, cities, and social circles would stop at once, and the world would be cured of many of its ills. If only we could learn, before passing on a bit of gossip, to ask that simple question "Is It Needful?" what a lot of heartaches we would save in this already overburdened life we live.

But perhaps the third gate of gold through which this old legend would force the witch to pass is most important of all, the gate of "Is It Kind?"

To test every piece of gossip by that phrase would abruptly stop most of the tragedy and unhappiness caused by unkind talk about our families, our friends, and our neighbors. That is the final gate through which all gossip should pass.

My friend Edwin Markham always refused to say an unkind word about anybody. He had his own motto and test. He used to say that he tested every deed of his life, particularly the deed of passing on gossip, by this simple question: "What is the loving thing to do?" He found that when he tested every deed and act and thought of his life by that phrase he did very few things which brought any unhappiness either to himself or to others. And "What is the loving thing to do?" was just another way of applying the third test of the Chinese legend, another way of making the old "Witch of Gossip" pass through the gate of "Is It Kind?"

❧　❧

A SORT OF ORDINATION

BENJAMIN WEST was a Quaker and a man of deep religious feeling. His occupation as a painter caused some misgivings among the strictest of the Quaker faith. To some it savored of vanity that a member of their society should give himself up to follow the frivolous art of painting. Very solemnly they called a meeting to discuss the matter. His unusual gifts and talents none could deny, and when one member arose and suggested that Benjamin's talent was undoubtedly a gift of God, they solemnly approved of his calling. Then very solemnly the members placed their hands upon his head and, in a sort of ordination service, prayed for God's blessing on his career as a painter. West never forgot that solemn hour and devoutly fulfilled their prayerful dedication.

As this famous painter said later: "One always does great work when he feels that his friends, his family, and his fellow churchmen are back of him with their hands in dedication on his brow. I could not let them down! I had to succeed!"

Yes, that is true of life in general. The man who knows that his wife is back of him; the woman who knows that a husband believes in her; children who know that their parents have faith in them; a president who knows that the people of the nation are praying for him, boosting him, loyally supporting him—these can do miracles in the world.

I remember a story Cecil De Mille once told me in Hollywood. When he was a nine-year-old boy, an old preacher came to Echo Lake, New Jersey, to conduct a series of meetings. Young Cecil De Mille attended every morning. But one cold, rainy morning he was the only person present. He wondered if that man would preach when only a small boy was present. He waited eagerly to see. And this is the way De Mille described the scene:

"If he preached under those circumstances I felt that he was a man of God. If he dismissed the service I felt that he would be false.

And he did preach, although it was a very short sermon. Then he came down to the altar railing of the church and invited me to come up. He said: "My audience no doubt noticed that I did not take the collection at the usual time. I now invite my audience to come up and put the offering in the plate."

I walked up proudly to that altar, put my nickle in the plate and, as I did so, that old gray-haired preacher put his hand on my head and prayed a prayer in which he lifted my name to God. I shall never forget the feel of that old preacher's hands on my head. I have enjoyed the greatest honors of life. Here in Hollywood I have met the great of the earth. But I have never had any thrill as great as the feel of that preacher's hands on my head. It was a kind of ordination. That had much to do with my interest in producing Biblical motion pictures.

There is no thrill, no encouragement, no impetus so great as the faith that others have in us!

ↄ　　ɔ

"HOW DEEP MAY I DRINK?"

LITTLE Hugh, one of seven children, met with a painful accident. Through the kindness of some friends of the family, he was taken to the hospital. Hugh came from a family so poor that his hunger was never quite satisfied.

After he was made as comfortable as possible in the hospital, the nurse brought him a glass of milk. Hugh looked at it longingly and then, with memory of many another glass of milk shared with his brothers and sisters, he said: "How deep may I drink?"

The nurse who sent me this story said she had to force back the tears as she answered, "Drink it all. Drink it all!"

We here in America have seldom had any restrictions on how deeply we may drink of the abundant life. We have had plenty of food, plenty of freedom, plenty of chances to carve out our own destinies. We have never had to ask how deeply we may drink of education, art, music, or beauty; for the radio has brought it all to us and in abundance. We have never had to ask how deeply we may drink of the physical, mental, or spiritual milk of life. We have had an abundance of vital raw resources for our own use and for the use of the world.

It is no small thing to have God's blessings in such abundance.

ↄ　　ɔ

THE LAMPS OF LOVE ARE SHINING

I HAVE a friend who collects old-fashioned lamps as a hobby. She happens to live in New England, so she searches through old homes, barns, outhouses, and ships for discarded and forgotten lamps—the type of lamps that some of us actually remember seeing our mothers clean and refill every morning.

I, for one, can see my mother take down the lamp, blow her breath into the thin glass globe and then wipe it out with a clean rag until it shines. I can see her trimming the black wicks with a pair of scissors; I can see her fill the lamp with pungent oil, which I still love to smell now and then when I happen into an old-time Cape Cod general grocery story where they still sell it in cans.

I remember the dirty potato that we used to stick on the end of the spout of the oilcan as we carried it home. I remember how my mother used to sit at nights in our West Virginia home and fashion old newspapers into long, narrow, pointed lighters. There was always a pile of them in the tall, red glass vase on our mantel. These lighters were used in the days when matches were expensive and scarce. They were stuck into the glowing, open fire on the hearth and used to light the lamps.

Time has changed all that, for with our electricity and our electric bulbs we do not worry much about light. We have been educated by radio, inventive ingenuity, and newspaper ads to protect our eyes and to use all of the electricity we need, without stint.

It was a delightful experience to visit my friend up in the New Hampshire Hills and see her collection of lamps, which she has in an old barn. She had cleaned and filled and lighted them all—more than three hundred of them—and the sight of those three hundred lamps burning in a deep, spacious old barn was as thrilling a sight as I have ever seen. The pungent smell of burning coal oil was a delight to the nostrils and to the memory. It conjured up the past and brought back romance as magically as Aladdin's lamp of ancient story.

And on the walls of that old New England barn was a little poem from the same ancient past that produced those old lamps. It was the most beautiful thing I got out of the day's visit and adventure. This is the poem, the author of which is long forgotten in the dust of New England history:

> My friends are little lamps to me,
> Their radiance warms and cheers my ways.
> And all my pathway, dark and lone,
> Is brightened by their rays.
> I try to keep them bright by faith,
> And never let them dim with doubt,
> For every time I lose a friend
> A little lamp goes out.

○   ○

"I AM STILL RICH"

A FRIEND of mine, in the midst of the late depression, wrote a little piece in his trade journal. I have been reading that piece recently, and it applies today as much as it did a few years ago. This is what he wrote then; and if he were living now, I feel certain that he would republish it:

We have passed through a panic, suffering from a crash on the stock market, and now more than half-way through the depression, I AM STILL RICH!

It may be true that I have much less to live on than I had a year ago, but it is certainly true that I have just as much as ever to live for.

My two hundred thousand dollar eyes are just as good as they ever were. Every landscape and sunset is mine if I want to take it. Twenty thousand dollar scenes and views are added to my collection almost every week! A hundred thousand dollar sense of hearing is still unimpaired and by it I become heir to a world of sound and beauty in the birds' singing at dawn, the wind in the trees, the far-off call of a whip-poor-will, the sound of a meadow lark, the beauty of a child's voice, the melody of a friend's greeting.

The depression has not lowered the value of a single friendship. Neighbors will still greet me in the same old cordial way, business associates still believe in me and my children still hold me in high affection. My wife's welcome at the close of the day has not depreciated in the least and my daughter still continues to lavish affection on me in the same old extravagant way.

The depression has cost us some of the things we created but it has robbed us of none of our power to create. We may lose some beautiful things but we have not lost our love for the beautiful.

It is a challenge, not a catastrophe. A generation that has conquered the air and sent giant planes circling the globe, which has plunged into the deeps and disported on the ocean's floor, which has climbed above the clouds and lived intimately in the stratosphere, is now faced with the challenge to rise above its dependence on mere things and seek an emancipation of the spirit of man.

The last years have been, for millions of men, a thrilling spiritual adventure; a calling forth of their courage, faith, stamina, a summoning of their hidden spiritual resources; a demand for sacrifice, service and spiritual power through which they have discovered their real wealth. Bereft of dividends and profits they have discovered the sustaining powers of a strong religious, personal, and national faith, the abiding values of courage, heroism, honor, charity and trustworthiness.

My personal friend David Beyer wrote that, and if he were alive today he would simply substitute the word "war" for "depression" and apply all of the fine philosophy to this day. Since he is not alive to do it I, who pass this gem on, and you who read it can make the contemporary application.

❦   ❧   ❧

"THE SLAYER LIES DEAD BY THE SLAIN"

EDWIN MARKHAM used to amuse himself in my home by writing little four-line poems, through which he could express a complete

99

thought. I doubt if there was ever a poet in the English-speaking world who wrote so many or such strong quatrains.

One day he read and presented to me for my own a little four-line poem which seems to me to have in it great hope for all of us. This is that quatrain:

> The robber is robbed by his riches;
> The tyrant is dragged by his chain;
> The schemer is snared by his cunning;
> The slayer lies dead by the slain.

Edwin Markham put the eternal philosophy of the inevitable end of tyranny in that simple quatrain—the fact that the very seeds of dissolution are bound up in tyranny.

> The robber is robbed by his riches;
> The tyrant is dragged by his chain;
> The schemer is snared by his cunning;
> The slayer lies dead by the slain.

How often have we watched this happen in small towns when we have seen the old Silas Marners of our villages die clutching the gold they accumulated through exploitation of the poor. How often have we seen men build their own Frankensteins and in the end have those very monsters crush them to death. How often have we seen a civilization create its own robots and then in turn seen, those robots turn and crush their own creators. There is hope for justice in a world where this can happen, and we do not need to have any great fear that injustice, the spirit of conquest, the cruel stalking of tyranny, will "at longlast survive." It carries the seeds of its own undoing.

ɔ   ɕ

SENSITIVE PLANTS

Not long ago *PM* in its Sunday issue had a full-page story of a sensitive plant which would respond to the most delicate outside movement. And to make that response more vivid the article was headed, "Even a Good Holler Scares These Sensitive Plants."

These sensitive plants have small, light blue flowers. To show how responsive they were to outside influences the author of that article said that the heat from a lighted match, a slight gust of air, or the heavy vibration of an automobile rumbling by would cause both the leaves and the flowers to collapse.

Some friends of mine were quite excited about this plant and its sensitivity, but it was no new story to me; for years ago when I used to visit Luther Burbank at Santa Rosa, California, he told me that all plants were sensitive; that they were so sensitive they would become unconscious in the presence of ether, just as a human being would. He said he would not employ a man who used alcohol, for plants were influenced even by the smell of alcohol. Nor would he employ anybody who smoked to help him in his delicate experimental work with plants.

Then he launched into one of his favorite themes. He said metals are the hardest things to change, that they require tremendous forces to mold them. To change gold you must employ a heavy hammer. Gold will resist acids and oxidation. To change iron you have to use tremendous heat and outside influences of every type. A plant will respond to the most delicate outside forces. But the most sensitive thing of all is a child. A child will respond to a thousand outside forces and influences that neither a plant nor a metal will feel. Therefore you can do with a child just about what you want to do, said the great plant scientist. You can make of a child by environment just about what you want to make of it. One of the phrases that Mr. Burbank used is this: "A child is as sensitive to outside influences and forces as a seismograph is sensitive to an earthquake which is ten thousand miles away, indicating its direction, its position, its center and its force."

Parents should see to it that only the most beautiful, character-developing, morale-creating influences touch that delicate sensitive plant we call a little child.

ↄ   ɔ

COME AND GET IT!

The gloom of the world is but a shadow. Behind it, yet within reach, is joy.

There is radiance and glory in the darkness, could we but see; and to see we have only to look.

I beseech you to look!

That sounds as if it might have been written yesterday, but it was actually written in 1513, by Fra Giovanni, a little after America was discovered. This present period of history is not the only dark period we have ever had. Nor is this period the only epoch in which we have had men of hope and religious faith.

This saintly man continued the letter to his friend by saying:

I am your friend and my love for you goes deep! There is nothing I can give which you have not got; but there is much, very much, that, while I cannot give you it, you can take. No heaven can come to us unless our hearts find rest in it today.

Take Heaven!

No peace lies in the future which is not hidden in the present instant. Take Peace!

Life is so generous a giver, but we, judging its gifts by the covering, cast them away as ugly or heavy or hard. Remove the covering and you will find beneath it a living splendor, woven of love, by wisdom, with power. Welcome it, grasp it and you touch the angel's hand that is there, and the wonder of an overshadowing presence. Our joys, too; be not content with them as joys. They too, concern diviner gifts.

Life, in spite of wars and rumors of wars; hurt and hate, gloom and darkness is so full of meaning and purpose, so full of beauty beneath its covering—that you will find earth but cloaks your heaven.

Courage then to claim it; that is all; but courage you have; and the knowledge that we are all pilgrims together, wending through this unknown country home! Now and forever, day breaks and the shadows flee away!

It is always comforting in these dark uncertain days to know that in other shadowed days there were men who could see light ahead; who knew as Fra Giovanni knew that "day breaks and the shadows flee away!"

⋄   ⋄

"IT OUGHT TO BE FINE! I LIVE HERE!"

MY friend Strickland Gillilan, who among other things gave to the world that unforgettable phrase

> Off ag'in, on ag'in,
> Gone a'gin.—FINNIGIN.

recently told me the story of a trip he took into the Deep South.

One day he was walking through the Negro section of a Southern city and was astonished at the neat way most of the residents of poor, run-down shacks in the Negro quarters kept their gardens.

One particular garden attracted his eye. It was laid out in a neat mosaic with a deep green against the black loam. Morning-glories twined around the unpainted boards of that shack. Roses twined over an unpainted wooden fence; sunflowers loomed and bloomed high about the Negro mammy who sat in an old rocking chair, mistress of all she surveyed. Strickland Gillilan paused, spoke to that old Negro woman and said: "A beautiful garden, mother."

She arose, cupped her hand to her good ear, and queried: "What you say, please, sir?"

"A beautiful garden!" he shouted back into her cupped hand.

"Sholy! It ought to be fine! I live here!"

That story hit me where I live. "It ought to be fine! I live here!" It is that type of pride which we in this nation need most of all at this time of world crisis.

Vachel Lindsay had it. It was his theory that a creative man should continue to live in the small town which was his home and make it worth living in. Therefore he refused to go to New York City when he first came to fame through his poems. And in Springfield he lived—with the exception of a year's teaching in the West—to the end. Once he expressed his philosophy in a poem called, "Make Springfield Beautiful." William Allen White has had that idea all of his life. He has remained in Emporia, Kansas, and helped to make Emporia beautiful and famous the world over.

Once when I was talking with Mr. White while he was in Boston to receive an honorary degree from Harvard he told me a good story. He was standing in an academic procession on a hot June day at Columbia. Another little man stood beside him. Mr. White, wanting to have a friendly conversation, said to the other man: "We ought to know each other. I'm a small town editor from Emporia, Kansas. My name is White." The man beside him replied: "I'm a small town doctor from Rochester, Minnesota, and my name is Mayo."

Each of them has made beautiful and worth while the small town in which he has lived for years, and the world has made a beaten pathway to each of their doors. Pride of home, no matter how humble; pride of family and clan; pride of citizenship in town, state, city or nation; pride of race; pride of religion—these are all immensely worth while. "It ought to be fine! I live here!"

❧   ☙

"FROM THE DAY YOU ARE BORN"

Mr. Luther Burbank, the world-famous scientist in plant breeding, was one day taking me through his laboratories in California. That day there had been a terrible cloudburst, and the rain had washed out several thousand experimental lily plants with which he had been working for years, trying to develop a black-petaled lily. I expressed sympathy over what had happened. Then he said something which I have never forgotten.

With a smile like a mischievous child he said: "When anything like this happens I always remember a little couplet my mother used to quote:

> From the day you are born till you ride in a hearse,
> There is nothing that happens which couldn't be worse.

Burbank chuckled and kept repeating that couplet over and over as we surveyed the damage the storm had done to his experimental lilies. Then he added with another chuckle:

Not many years ago Mark Twain visited me here. We were talking about that very thought, and Mark told us a story. He said: "One day a neighbor came to my home in the East with his face all wrapped up in a rag. He evidently had the toothache and wanted sympathy. I looked at him and laughed at the expression on his face. Then, a little hurt at my apparent lack of sympathy, that neighbor said: 'Laugh if you must, but I have both the toothache and the headache. Can you imagine anything worse?' I replied to him: 'Yes, it would be worse to have muscular rheumatism and the St. Vitus' Dance.'"

Then Mr. Burbank added: "Yes,

> From the day you are born till your ride in a hearse,
> There is nothing that happens which couldn't be worse."

And Mr. Burbank is right.

We talk a good deal today about our many taxes, and we get to feeling imposed upon, harassed, and exploited. But just a moment. Here is the answer: We are taxed mildly compared with Germany, England, Italy—almost any nation on the face of the earth. Here is the next answer: We have our world series; our outdoor boxing matches under moonlit skies; our summer music festivals in every great American city—these we enjoy without fear of dive bombers or bursting shells.

A little stray verse contains a plaintive story about a man who had lost his all—his house, his job, his money. He had no clothes, no food, no shoes. But, as he put it,

Then suddenly I felt myself ashamed!
For I, who talked of shoes, then chanced to meet
A man who had no feet!

Yes, no matter what your problem is,

From the day you are born till you ride in a hearse,
There is nothing that happens which couldn't be worse.

❂   ❂

THE BRIDGE BENT, BUT IT DID NOT BREAK

ONE of America's greatest builders of bridges is L. A. Paddock, president of the American Bridge Company. It was his company that built the great Golden Gate Bridge.

One of my most vivid memories is that of sitting with him in my home and talking about the great bridges of the world. He used to tell me about a great bridge that would some day be built across Sydney Harbor. In fact, he spent a year studying the problem and bidding on that bridge for his company. Then he talked about a great bridge that would some day be built across the river at Detroit, connecting Detroit with Canada. Once he said a thing which I have never forgotten. "Great bridges are built in some engineer's mind." Then we got to talking about the bridge at the Golden Gate in San Francisco, and I remember with what certainty he told me that, as impossible as it then seemed, one day those bridges would be built.

I crossed those bridges several times when I visited the great fair in San Francisco.

The year before I visited San Francisco a hurricane hit the California coast, climaxing two weeks of stormy weather, causing wide-spread damage and many deaths. I read in the newspaper dispatches that the thirty-five million dollar Golden Gate Bridge bent twelve and one-half feet out of line under the terrific force of that wind, which reached a speed of seventy-five miles an hour.

When I came home I reminded my friend of that newspaper story, and this is what he said: "Yes, it bent, but it did not break, for that bridge was built to sway as much as eighteen feet under wind pressure. It bent, but it did not break."

It is not unusual for men, women, things, or nations to bend under the blasts of life, but it is tragic if they break. Institutions and men and women are expected to bend, but they are not expected to break, as an Oregon bridge once did, unless there has been some flaw in their plans or characters. I love to look upon the old cedar trees of the Monterey Coast, which have through the years been bent until they almost touch the ground. But they have not broken.

＊　＊

"IF HE CAN WIN, THEN I CAN TOO"

NOT long ago Mrs. Eleanor Roosevelt said in a public address in my hearing. "Every time another man or woman rises above what seems to be an insurmountable difficulty and wins out, I feel that every one of us should get a lift. If he can win, then I can too!"

It was most natural for all of us who sat at that banquet table—and I was fortunate enough to be sitting beside Mrs. Roosevelt—to think of her own husband. I do not know that she did, but I thought I heard a new fiber in her very tones as she made that statement. I remembered that my friend Angela Morgan, in a tribute to President Roosevelt and his courage after being stricken with paralysis, said of him:

> I ask no truce, I have no qualms,
> I seek no quarter and no alms:
> Stand forth my soul, and grip thy woe:
> Buckle thy sword and face thy foe!
> Do others fear, do others fail?
> My soul will grapple and prevail!

I do not know what she was thinking, but I thought of another great man, a citizen of Illinois. At the age of twenty-two, after seven years of hard work, he found that the sheriff had tacked a sign on the door of his store. And he realized that he was penniless. After saving up for two years to pay his debts, he tried another partner, only to see his savings swept away the second time, with another crushing debt facing him.

Then his partner died, leaving him to shoulder the burden. But he paid the whole debt. At thirty he started again as a surveyor and had to borrow money to get his instruments and a horse.

Shortly after this, the girl he loved died suddenly. This seemed too much, and he was on the verge of insanity through sheer grief. His friends dared not leave him alone but nursed him back to mental poise and health. Ten years later he tried politics again and secured the nomination to Congress, but failed, and in two more years his constituents returned him to Congress. Nine years later his friends had him nominated for the Senate. But at the last moment he had to yield to his oponent; he had failed again. Two years later he made one more attempt to attain the Senatorship, meeting his haughty and condescending opponent in a series of debates, which history still remembers and which made immortal the towns in which they took place. But again he went down in defeat. Thirty years now of constant and sincere effort and thirty years of failure and defeat. He might have been forgiven if he had forsaken the fight. At fifty he was down and out, seemingly for good, with deep furrows in his face.

Then two years later, with one last heroic effort, that Illinois man ran for the Presidency of this nation and was elected! The world now knows the story of Abraham Lincoln, and when we remember that story we say, with Mrs. Roosevelt: "If he can win, then I can too."

HOW MOODY AND SANKEY MET

MOODY AND SANKEY were the most famous pair of evangelistic workers who ever lived, and out of this combination came the famous popular hymn "The Ninety and Nine" in a London meeting. That story of Sankey's cutting the words out of a newspaper and improvising the tune is too well known to tell again, but the story of how they met is worth recalling and retelling.

Moody was preaching in his Chicago church on Illinois Street when the great Chicago fire broke out and swept on toward his church, but he continued his sermon. Moody's church was destroyed that night, and several of his church members were killed in other parts of the devastated area.

Shortly after the fire, Mr. Moody went to Indianapolis to attend the International Convention of the Y. M. C. A.

Another young man was there from Pennsylvania. He was an officer in the Internal Revenue Service with a salary of fifteen hundred dollars a year, he could sing beautifully. Sankey had heard of "that young evangelist from Chicago," so when he arrived in Indianapolis, he hunted Moody up. They liked each other from the start.

During the convention it was announced that "Mr. Moody from Chicago" would conduct a prayer meeting at six o'clock in a little room some distance from the Academy of Music. That "some distance" turned out to be miles away, and Sankey didn't reach the "little room" until Moody was half-way through his talk.

The Rev. Robert McMillen, who happened to know Sankey, saw him enter the room and asked him to sing something when Mr. Moody was through. He was ready, and the minute that Moody was through he arose, without announcement, and sang:

> There is a fountain filled with blood
>   Drawn from Immanuel's veins;
> And sinners plunged beneath that flood,
>   Lose all their guilty stains.

A hush fell over that crowd. Mr. Moody was deeply touched,

ran down from the platform, put his arms around Sankey, and said: "Where are you from?"

"Pennsylvania," replied Sankey.

"Married or single?" asked Moody in sharp, machine-gun-like words.

"Married. I have a wife and one child."

"What do you do for a living?"

"I am in the government service," replied Sankey, mystified.

All this time Moody was holding Sankey's hand as if determined not to let him get away. Looking down into his face with his keen black eyes, Moody said:

"Well, you'll have to give it up and come with me. You are just the man I'm looking for. You'll do the singing, and I'll do the talking. Chicago is waiting for us! Come on, man! God needs us!"

That is exactly what Sankey did, and thus was born the greatest combination of evangelism that ever got together, a combination which changed the religious history of the world, wrote the most dramatic chapter in evangelistic missions, and gave to the world one of its greatest hymns, "The Ninety and Nine."

ɔ   ɕ

"I'LL BE SEEING YOU"

AT the funeral of Marie Dressler, the lovable Hollywood star, who bound us all to her heart by dint of her humaneness and her lovely characterizations, there were literally thousands of floral tributes. But there was one which impressed me more than all the others put together, and that one came from Alice Brady. It bore the inscription "Au Revoir," and beneath that were these words: "I'll be seeing you, Marie."

The implication of immortality in that phrase intrigued me. Alice Brady knew that that was not the end of her friendship with Marie Dressler. She knew that somewhere, sometime, she would be seeing her again.

Several years ago, I had a young student whom I loved. He fell ill with tuberculosis after a brilliant career as a minister. I visited him every day for six months in a Boston hospital. Then one day I went to see him, and the doctors told me that he could live for only a few hours. They had not told Bob Ropp that he was near death, and I wondered whether he had guessed.

A word of prayer, and I felt that I ought to go because he was so weak. I took his hand and said, "Now, Bob, I must go. I have to catch a train for California in an hour."

A new light came into his eyes, a slight twinkle, a look of assurance and certainty, and he said: "All right, Prof. Good-by— and I'll be seeing you!"

Then I knew that he knew. His youthful spirit was telling me through that universal slang slogan that he too believed in immortality and that if he did not see me on this earth again he would see me in the Great Tomorrow. I can still hear the ring of absolute confidence in his voice as he said with a smile, "Good-by, Prof. I'll be seeing you!"

ઙ   ଓ

KEEPING THE SOUL OF THINGS ALIVE

PEOPLE who know their Bible stories will like this pleasant little story about Zacchaeus, the small, insignificant-looking tax collector, who climbed into a tree so that he could see Jesus one day when he was passing. As a result of that experience Jesus befriended this despised man, restored his self-respect, and saved his soul.

The story has it that when Zacchaeus was an old man he still dwelt in Jericho, humble and pious. Every morning at sunrise he went out into the fields for a walk and came back with a calm and happy mind, no matter in what mood he went forth. After that, he was ready to begin his day's work with strength and courage.

His wife wondered where he went on those walks, but he never spoke to her of the matter. So, being curious, as most women are, she followed him one morning.

He went straight to the tree from which he had first seen Jesus on that immortal morning when he found a new friend and found his own soul. Taking a large urn to a near-by spring, he filled it with water, carried it to the tree, and poured it around the roots, which were getting dry in that hot climate. He pulled up all the weeds around the tree. Then he looked up among the branches where he had sat that day when he first saw the Lord; and a new light of peace and contentment came into his old eyes. He turned away with a smile of gratitude and went back to his work.

Zacchaeus knew in his soul that he wanted to keep the spirit of that unusual experience alive, and to do so he tried to keep the tree alive. How true that necessity is in everyday life!

We have to make some definite effort to keep the worth-while things of life alive, especially the spiritual things of religion, friendship, beauty, and love; for they are delicate plants and need attention.

This is particularly true of love. People fall in love, get married, start a home; and then they take things for granted and make no special effort to keep alive that "first fine careless rapture" of love. But wise people tend that plant, water it, keep the weeds of misunderstandings out, cultivate it, and reap a great reward of happiness and peace in so doing.

It is so with friendship and religion. Often men have very definite religious experiences, but if they fail to water and cultivate those experiences they are as apt to die out as any other experience of life. Zacchaeus even went so far as to try to keep alive the very tree under which he met the Lord of Life. It is worth thinking about.

☽　　　☾

LIFE'S INDESTRUCTIBLES

DICK LEHNER is a real American boy who lives in Kansas City. He is a regular boy and as sturdy as an oak. He sings in the choir in Grace and Holy Trinity Church. He was on his way home from school one day when some of the boys told him that a disastrous fire had completely destroyed the wonderful pipe organ, choir loft, and altar of his church. It was just before Easter, and Dick and the boy singers had been practicing for weeks to give the beautiful Easter music in that very chancel. Dick was brokenhearted.

When he got home he called Miss Mabelle Glenn, the choir director, to ask about the bad news he had just heard. There he stood at the phone. He had been playing marbles; his face was dirty and streaked with perspiration; his cap was on the side of his head, the bill over his left ear, anxiety written all over his grim and anxious face.

When the choir director appeared at the phone Dick asked her if the bad news was true, and she told him that it was; that the beautiful organ, chancel, and choir loft were destroyed; that there would be no Easter service and singing there.

After waiting a fraction of a second, Dick gulped hard, had a bewildered look in his eyes, as his mother tells me of it, and then said: "G'bye, Miss Glenn, I guess I'm gonna cry."

Tears coursed down his dirty cheeks, sobs shook his boyish frame. Then he wiped his nose across his sleeve, pulled himself together, dabbed at his eyes in typical boy fashion, turned to his mother and said: "That won't lick us, and it won't lick me. We'll just keep goin' on as if that fire hadn't happened."

Then he called Miss Glenn back and said, "I'm O.K. now. I ain't cryin' any more! When do we practice?"

I like that story out of real life. I like it because it comes out of the heart of a typical and real American boy. I like it because it typifies the American spirit. I like it because it is in the spirit of a story I recently read in the *Woman's Home Companion* written by the Rev. Michael Coleman, vicar of All Hallows Church in London, near Tower Hill, which American tourists like to visit because it is close to the famous London Tower. That church was destroyed completely by bombs. But its rector, the morning after its destruction, started in on a program of serving his people without any church. In his article he gave an outline of what he was doing from dawn to midnight every day. And it was a thrilling story.

But the title was what got me. He called his story "The Indestructible Church." It reminded me that there is something indestructible about the human spirit from boys to men, from preachers to soldiers.

❧   ❧

"LIKE SILVER IN THE SUN"

GRACE NOLL CROWELL is perhaps the most popular woman poet in America today. Sometimes she gets as many as five hundred letters a week from people whom her poems have helped. They come from all over the world, but most of them come from hospital beds where people are suffering through diseases and accidents. She seems to write mostly for them. Why? Because she herself has been an invalid since her first son was born, and she has spent more than half of her useful life in hospitals and confined to her home. She has walked where the ill have walked, and she knows.

She told me the outstanding memory of her childhood. One day, when she was a small child, she was cleaning pewter pots for her mother. As she rubbed and cleaned, suddenly she cried out to her mother in an ecstasy of joy: "O Mother, I glittered it! I glittered it!"

Her mother smiled and said: "All right, darling, go on and glitter it some more!"

Then the little girl continued her polishing, talking to the pewter pot as she rubbed, saying over and over to that dull pot: "I'll glitter you! I'll glitter you! I'll make you shine like silver in the sun! I'll make you shine like silver in the sun!"

And that is exactly what Mrs. Crowell has been doing all her life. She has been making things and places and people shine like silver in the sun. She has been making her life and home do the same thing.

One day she was broadcasting on a Dallas, Texas, station. It was a Christmas program, and when it was all over the manager said to Mrs. Crowell: "Now since we are not paying you and you have made so many people happy, we want to give you the gift you would like most of all. What do you want most of all this Christmas?"

Mrs. Crowell thought a moment and then said: "Oh, I want a new rug for my back bedroom. The old one is worn to the nap."

"You shall surely have that," replied the manager. "But now tell me something spiritual that you would rather have than anything else in the world."

Mrs. Crowell replied: "Peace! Peace for all people who have lonely, hurt bodies and hearts! Peace for the world, our poor, tired, hurt old world."

And that will suggest to my readers why it is that this much-loved poet is able to go about making life shine "like silver in the sun."

ා   ල

THIS BOY FACES HIS OWN WEAKNESSES

RECENTLY I received a letter from a boy who was discharged from the army because he couldn't face the discipline. It is a letter which has courage and resolution in it, and it has much to do with explaining the so-called high morale in the army and nation. All that this boy says is true of himself and true of many others. He has been a problem to himself, to his teachers, and to his parents for many years; but there seems to be hope ahead for him. Here is the letter:

The past year has seen a decidedly unbalancing effect on my morals, which were never the best. As you probably know, I was recently discharged from the army as a result of what is technically known as "Psychoneurosis." It is probably true that I am more sensitive to certain things than the average person. However, I have had a great deal of time to think things out during the past months, and there are many things about myself that I am unable to condone or excuse on the grounds of my being more "sensitive," more intelligent, or better educated than those who stand the gaff of life better than I do.

The unpalatable but stark truth of the matter is that I have become soft and flabby through too many years of self-indulgence and avoidance of reality. In this I am undoubtedly not alone.

It is one of the primary evils of my generation that it has lost the moral courage and the physical and mental standing to accept and fight its way out of difficulties. For the sake of America and the world I hope there are not many like myself.

It is somewhat futile to try to place the blame for the weakness of the youth of today. Perhaps we're all to blame—parents, teachers, politicians, and youth itself—for the acceptance of a code that places security above freedom and leisure above labor.

Most of us are inclined to be too lenient with ourselves and too harsh on others. When every man begins to sweep in front of his own door, maybe we'll have a cleaner world.

I, like many others, have been spoiled by easy living, and now the time has come to pay the reckoning. If, at some future date, when I have shown to myself and those in authority that I can adequately respond to the demands of ordinary living, maybe the army will be willing to give me another chance. Should that day arrive, I will consider it a privilege, not an imposition, to serve in whatever capacity I may be most useful.

❧　　❧

A THANKSGIVING MONTH GAME

I HAVE a little game I like to play with my friends every November as we approach Thanksgiving time. I write at least one of what I call "Thanksgiving letters" every day in November.

I write that letter to somebody to whom I am truly thankful for something he has contributed to my life in the past and whom I have never stopped to thank. Years ago I started out with my parents. I wrote them letters thanking them for all the beautiful, helpful things they had contributed to my life when I was a child, a young man, and even into middle age.

Then I wrote to my closest friends, one by one. Here was one friend who had introduced me to the works of Tennyson, Browning, Dickens; another friend who had spoken a wise word to me at a crucial time in my life. I wrote to all of my old teachers, from grammar school through high school and college. Sometimes a letter went to a cobbler, a grocer, a newsboy. Sometimes one went to a banker in my home town or to a streetcar conductor. One went to a high-school football coach, whose address I found one day in the newspapers because he had done a heroic act in saving a child from drowning.

There is no limit to the number of people to whom these letters can be sent if one sits down and thinks about those who have made some distinctive contribution to his life. The tragedy of it is that we accept these contributions and never think to offer a word of thanks for them.

One of the most beautiful things about this little game is the rich treasure house of letters we get in return. People who had long since forgotten us are thrilled by them. Teachers who have retired and who are sitting alone and lonely in some secluded room, forgotten by the world, are given a new lease on life by those "thank you" letters, and they are eternally grateful for the heartening word we send them. I have a big file of the letters I have received in answer to my Thanksgiving letters through the years.

I did not start out this little November game for the sake of receiving letters. In fact, I was only doing it to satisfy my own soul, but the by-products of writing those letters have enriched my own life immeasurably. Now when I get to feeling blue and need a little lift I read those letters over and am heartened and refreshed by them. One such letter I received this last year. It came from Mrs. Wentworth, a high-school teacher, whom I had thanked for inspiring in me a love for Tennyson. This is her letter:

Dear Willie:

I am an old lady in my eighties. I am ill and cannot leave my room. Your letter came like a ray of bright sun, illuminating my dark day and my even darker life. You will be interested to know that, after fifty years of teaching, yours was the first letter of thanks I ever received from a former student. You lifted the clouds for me.

ᕉ   ᕒ

AN OLD HYMN COMES ALIVE AGAIN

ONE of the most popular hymns ever written is Cardinal Newman's "Lead, Kindly Light."

Most of us oldsters remember that the hymn found a new popularity in this nation when William McKinley was shot by an assassin, for it was this president's favorite hymn. Millions of men and women sang it the day of his funeral. I myself have never been trained as a singer, but that is one hymn I know—every note, pause, emphasis, and intonation. I can sing it perfectly, because in my home town, Moundsville, West Virginia, as a boy I was invited to join a quartet to learn that hymn and to sing it at a McKinley Memorial Service. We were trained for a week and were all letter- and note- perfect in that single hymn. To this day, when I swing into that old hymn, I do so confidently and with joy.

John Henry Newman was born February 21, 1801, the son of a London banker. Graduated from Trinity College, Oxford, he was ordained to the ministry in 1824, and became the Vicar of St. Mary's Protestant Episcopal Church in 1827. However, through the spiritual unrest kindled by the first Oxford Movement, Dr. Newman, as many a prominent writer and public character has done in recent days of unrest—including Arnold Bennett, Alfred

118

Noyes and Heywood Broun—decided to unite with the Catholic Church. He did so in 1845. He became cardinal in 1879.

Cardinal Newman himself tells of how that great hymn happened to be written:

My health had suffered from the labours involved in the composition of my volume. . . . I was easily persuaded to join Hurrell Froude and his father, who were going to the south of Europe for the health of the former. . . . I went down at once to Sicily, . . . I struck into the middle of the island, and fell ill of a fever at Leonforte. My servant thought that I was dying, and begged for my last directions. I gave them, as he wished; but I said: "I shall not die." I repeated, "I shall not die, for I have not sinned against light, I have not sinned against light!" . . . Towards the end of May I set off for Palermo, . . . Before starting from my inn in the morning of May 26th or 27th, I sat down on my bed and began to sob bitterly. My servant, who acted as my nurse; asked what ailed me. I could only answer, "I have a work to do in England." . . . At last I got off in an orange boat bound for Marseilles. We were becalmed a whole week in the Straits of Bonifacio. Then it was that I wrote the lines "Lead, kindly light" (June 16, 1833).

Dr. John B. Dykes composed the music to that great hymn as he walked through the Strand, one of the busiest thoroughfares of London. Today the hymn is coming into a new popularity, because it expresses a great need of the human heart in the dark days of war.

"Lead, kindly Light, amid the encircling gloom."

☙　❧

APPLE-BLOSSOM TIME

A YOUNG girl who was engaged kept a little black book as her diary. One day she wrote in it: "When the apple blossoms are in bloom we will be married."

And sure enough she and her young banker were married at apple-blossom time and in an old apple orchard. It was as she had wished from girlhood. She was dressed in a white satin dress—her mother's wedding dress. There was a gloriously happy look in her eyes; and there was a proud, possessive look in the tanned face of the groom.

They took their honeymoon in a shiny new buggy with a chestnut horse which belonged to the groom. The first paragraph in the girl's diary after the honeymoon was an ecstatic note about their trip "in apple blossom time." Later items in the book tell of failures and successes; joys and sorrows; even a few domestic misunderstandings now and then. But that diary also tells of how every year "at apple-blossom time" the young couple visited some beautiful apple orchard where they could renew their vows. When their savings were large enough, they would dine afterward at some remote hotel or quaint restaurant. But when there had been illness in the family, and the budget had to be carefully prepared, there were sandwiches and a thermos jug of coffee.

After several years they had two children, and those children soon learned to anticipate with joy and delight the "anniversary outing" of their mother and father. But one year when the children were in school, the parents decided to go on a week-end visit for their celebration. When they arose that morning, they found the following note on the breakfast table: "Dear Mother and Dad, us kids are glad you are married today. Have a good time and come back to us."

Thirty-three anniversary trips have been recorded in the "little black book." The children have homes of their own now. But each year that gray-haired father and mother make their annual pilgrimage together, and a new light is kindled in their faces as they keep this sacred tryst "at apple-blossom time."

ꙅ   ට

CHARACTER COUNTS!

BOSTON COLLEGE always has a great football team. One year recently they had one of the best in this nation, for they were selected to play the Sugar Bowl game.

Between halves the "Eagles" were trailing with a 7-0 margin. Things didn't look any too well. The weather was warm, and they were not used to southern humidity and heat. In the first half they had made about every blunder that could be made.

As the players waited between halves for Coach Leahy they talked over what he might possibly say to them. They had a guess that he would take them apart one by one. They knew they deserved it. Most coaches would have. Also there were some who thought that he might give them some heroics and hysterics—an inspirational pep talk about the good old Alma Mater; what Boston was expecting of them; what some of their favorite priests and teachers back at the college were hoping from them. But he did none of those things, according to the reports the boys made after they had turned in that phenominal come-back, that spectacular last minute win which gave them a certain immortality in football annals.

Coach Leahy came into that dressing room quietly, looked them over with a sympathetic and understanding eye, and then said something like this:

"Fellows, you're in here discouraged, upset, and all tired out. I don't blame you for anything. You're weary with this unexpected heat. The humidity has been terrific, and the game has been hard. You're behind, and it doesn't seem as if you could last another thirty minutes."

They felt their hearts warming up to him again. He certainly wasn't doing the orthodox and expected thing.

"But you're not discouraged because you men have character! Character is the great factor in this game or in any game. It will keep you going harder in the face of adversity. Character will decide this game; and you men have that!"

A hush fell over those tired men. The room was still. One of the players said after the game: "As I listened, I knew that Coach Leahy had confidence in us. I myself began to feel inside of me something that gave me new life. And we won!"

❧   ❧

SPELLING GOD WITH THE WRONG BLOCKS

THEODORE ROOSEVELT was one of Edwin Arlington Robinson's greatest admirers. In 1905, when Roosevelt was president, he wrote an enthusiastic review of Robinson's poetry, and that review helped to gain for Robinson a great audience.

Critics often argued over Robinson's philosophy. One critic wrote: "His humor is of a grim sort, and the world is not beautiful to him, but a prison-house."

Rollo Walter Brown, the novelist and essayist, was closer to Robinson than most men. Both of them did their writing at the MacDowell Colony in Peterboro, New Hampshire. Rollo Brown walked and talked with Robinson every summer and found him to be a cheerful, friendly, warm-hearted man. However, he was a realist, and it was because of his realism that he got the reputation of being hard and cynical.

One day Mr. Brown asked him about the criticism that had just been published, and Robinson replied: "I am sorry to learn that I have painted myself in such dark colors. The world is not 'a prison-house' as my critic says I think it is, but a kind of spiritual kindergarten, where millions of bewildered infants are trying to spell 'God' with the wrong blocks."

Robinson was as nearly right as any man can be with a simple figure of speech or a symbol. We are a lot of bewildered children in a kindergarten, trying to spell "God" but using the wrong blocks. But I have another symbol which will clear up this confusion.

A child was trying to put together a puzzle. On one side of the puzzle was a map of the world. There were hundreds of pieces to it, and he was having a confusing time. Then the boy's father came along and discovered that on the other side of that puzzle was a portrait of Christ. He said to the young son: "Why don't you turn it over and try to piece together first the picture of Christ?" The boy did as his father suggested, and soon he had put together the simple painting of the Christ. After that it was easy to get together the world on the other side.

The minute we learn that the spirit of Christ will help us to understand God, that minute shall we be a happier people and a peaceful world. My friend Edwin Markham once said:

> Here is the truth in a little creed,
> Enough for all the ways we go.
> In Love is all the Law we need;
> In Christ is all the God we know.

In spite of every attempt to relegate the Christ to obscurity, the fact still remains that the world will be a happier world only when the spirit of Christ binds us together and helps us to see God.

ᗧ   ᗣ

THE STARS ARE STILL THERE

MANY people in these desperate and uncertain days—mothers whose sons have been taken off to war; fathers whose hopes have been shattered; boys themselves whose lives have been abruptly broken into—all get to feeling that the things which matter most are at the mercy of the things which matter least. But this is not so.

The fields of wheat and corn in the Midwest are still growing in the same old way; the glorious splashing, golden crimson sunsets still come nightly to the skies; spring, summer, autumn, and winter still run their destined cycles; young couples are still getting married.

Babies are still being born in the same old way in which they have been born since "Adam delved and Eve span"; through travail and suffering; glow and glory.

Wild flowers are still blooming, and birds are still nesting and singing. The world has not come to an end; the skies have not fallen; God is still in his heaven, even though all is not exactly right with the world.

Dan Crawford used to sit in his African tent, homesick for England as he watched the earth darken and the stars come out, and say to himself, "God only hides a world to unveil a Universe." And he was comforted that the universal laws were still at work.

My friend Brashear, the noted astronomer of Pittsburgh, said on the day he died, when a friend asked him if he were not afraid to go out into the unknown, "I have loved the stars too fondly to be fearful of the night."

There is a legend from China which I picked up years ago. Two surveyors were crossing a trackless desert. They had a map showing certain trees, streams, and contours of land which they were to follow. But one night a terrible storm came. They hid in a cave, and when morning came all the landmarks had been swept or washed away. They were lost. Both of them were desperate. Their maps were useless, for every landmark shown on them had been destroyed by the storm. All day long they tried to figure out a way to safety. They dared not leave that cave and slept there the second night. About midnight one surveyor ran into the cave crying out, "We're saved! We can find our way through this desolation!"

"How?" his friend asked, thinking that he had gone crazy.

"Because the stars are still there!" his friend replied.

In these dark days of uncertainty, when most of the ancient landmarks have been swept away, the stars are still there. The real things of life, the universal laws of God, still survive. The stars are still there, my friends—the stars of love, hope, faith, prayer, communion with God, home, sacrifice, loyalty, and courage!

124

LOVE AND LOYALTY WILL LIFT ANY LOAD

A FEW days ago I walked across the Harvard yard with Rollo Walter Brown, one of this nation's famous novelists, who is also a professor at Harvard. He took me into Appleton Chapel and showed me that glorious memorial erected to the Harvard boys who died in the first World War. I cast my eye down the list. Here are three names that I particularly noticed: Quentin Roosevelt, son of "Teddy" Roosevelt; James Fenimore Cooper, Jr.; and Lioner de Jersey Harvard, the only member of the Harvard family in England ever to attend Harvard University.

Then I heard one of the most beautiful stories I ever heard from Rollo Brown.

It seems that young Harvard came to America in 1911. After graduating, four years later, he returned to England and enlisted. One night he was in the trenches near the Somme Line, and all night long he talked about his college to an Englishman who stood beside him in the trenches. That comrade says that he never saw young Harvard's face that dark night in the trenches as they stood watch, but he remembers his beautiful, well-modulated voice and his enthusiasm for the American college as he talked in the night.

The shells whined through the darkness; the very lights arose gracefully over No Man's Land—too far away to light up young Johnny Harvard's face. But his comrade never forgot that voice and that boy's loyalty to his college. The next day Johnny Harvard was brought in—dead. His English friend then saw his face.

In 1921, President Lowell, of Harvard, received a letter from that Englishman who had stood in the trenches that night with Johnny Harvard. The Englishman was writing to President Lowell to ask if he might send his two sons to Harvard. He had never been in the United States and had never seen Harvard. He said that his family up to that time had always gone to Oxford; but that, one night in the trenches, he met a young man named Harvard, who talked to him with such pride about his college in America—talked so loyally and so lovingly of that college—that

125

now, since his own sons were old enough to go to college, he wondered if it might be possible to send them to that college of which the boy had spoken.

Beneath that memorial is this inscription: "While a bright future beckoned, they freely gave their lives and fondest hopes for us and for our allies, that we might learn from them courage in peace, to spend our lives making a better world for others." I came away from that Melvina Hoffman Memorial with the feeling that love and loyalty to any institution—a college, a home, a fraternal organization, or a nation—is one of the most beautiful of all human traits. Such love and a loyalty makes a better world for others.

⊃   ⊂

"WHEN HE KNOWS IT'S ME . . ."

A CERTAIN mother, knowing how much I am interested in children and young people and knowing my interest in family life and what it means to America—its loyalties, its solidarity, its spirit of sacrifice—sent me a story that has thrilled me beyond expression. This is the way she tells it out of her simple home life:

Ronald, my boy, who had his fifteenth birthday just yesterday, was busy one evening making an airplane. I heard a knock at the door and when I went to the door there stood a boy and he asked if "Ron" could come out for a minute.

"Ronald doesn't loiter around much and when I told him he was wanted at the front door of our home, he asked me who it was.

"I don't know. He didn't give me his name." I replied.

"What kind of a sweater has he on?"

"I didn't notice."

"What color is his hair?"

"I didn't notice that either."

"Is he tall or short?"

"Medium."

"Tell him I'm too busy to come out tonight. I'm building an airplane." Ronald finally said to me.

126

I went back and told the boy that Ronald had said that he was too busy to come out; and then what a look of disappointment on his face; but quick as a flash what a joyous light spread over that boy's face and what a ring of confidence came into his voice as he said: "When Ron knows it's me, he won't be too busy to come out!"

Then immediately that boy sprang to the window and rapping on it he yelled: "Hi! Ron! It's me! Come on out!"

I shall never forget that ring of confidence in that boy's voice as he said: "When he knows it's me he won't be too busy."

When I received that letter I had just read of the bombing of St. Paul's Cathedral in London. St. Paul's means much to the English-speaking people, but to me it means just one thing. It is the cathedral in which I first saw that magnificent painting "Behold I Stand at the Door and Knock." It shows the Christ with a lantern in his hand knocking at a closed door. There is no latch outside of that door, symbolic of the fact that it cannot be opened from outside. It can only be opened from within, but Christ's face seems to be saying, in the words of this boy-story, "When he knows it's me he won't be too busy to come out."

❧　☙

OUR UNIVERSAL ROSARIES

THE Catholic Church has given humankind many beautiful symbols and rituals which have enriched our lives immensely. The Protestant churches and the Jewish faith share these symbolisms, and the most beautiful of them all is the rosary. We all like to think of the beautiful symbolism of counting our rosaries of faith, of friendship, and of memory.

There is no more popular song of modern times than "The Rosary"; and "Ave Maria" has stirred the hearts of men for untold years.

One day when I was interviewing Frank Murphy, of the Supreme Court, he told me a story of how his mother used to take him to church. He was just a boy of ten; but he tells me that as he sat in church, not knowing what it was all about, watching his mother count her beads on her rosary, something beautiful and sacred crept into his heart which has influenced his life all through the eventful, adventuring, and successful years.

We all have our spiritual rosaries to count. We have our rosaries of memories, and they are beautiful. Someone has said "Memories were given us that we might have red roses in December." What a beautiful and comforting thing it is to keep those memories fresh and green by counting them over in the twilight hours! No life in old age can be unhappy if that life has kept its most glowing memories fresh and green by counting them over in the twilight hours. That is one reason we should build beautiful memories into our lives—the memory of a great book; a beautiful poem; a glorious sunset; a spring that came bursting into life one immortal dawn in childhood when the lilacs first bloomed; the locust trees that sprang into blossom over night; the time we heard the first call of a bobwhite, a meadow lark, or a robin. Memory is one rosary we can count in our silent moments.

Then there is the rosary of great thoughts which have come to us. All along the hard ways of life we find great thoughts. They stir us to our depths. Then they somehow escape us. But they do not escape those who make a habit of memorizing beautiful things and thoughts. Those wise persons have a rosary of great thoughts to refresh them when dark days come.

However, to me the most beautiful rosary of all is what I call the rosary of friendship, and somewhere I have found an elusive little verse of four lines which I like to send out to my friends and to run over in my mind when I feel blue and unhappy, baffled and bewildered. I wish I knew who wrote it, and perhaps this publication will help me to find the author:

> Always when the old year ends,
> I clasp my rosary of friends,

128

And pause to breathe a grateful prayer
For every bead of friendship there.

When I count my rosaries of memory, of great thoughts, of kindly deeds which I have done and which have been done to me, and my rosary of friendship, I get more out of life.

☙　❧

MORE VALUABLE THAN MUCH FINE GOLD

THE ancient Talmud tells the story of a king who had a dream. And in his dream he saw a huge pair of scales held in the hand of Justice. The scales seemed to reach from earth to sky. In one side of the scales was a pile of gold, jewels, lumber, houses, lands —all symbols of earthly, material power. In the other side of the scales was a nest of straw. The gold, jewels, houses, and lands had tipped the scales down until the nest of straw was high in the air, and the gold-laden side of the scales touched the earth.

Then some guardian angel robed in white came along with a child in her arms and put that little child in the nest of straw. The King in his dream saw the scales immediately begin to move until the child outweighed the side laden with gold, jewels, houses, and lands. Yes, the side with the child touched the earth, and the material side tipped to the sky.

"That means," said the king to himself, "that the most valuable thing on this earth is a little child. The child outweighs them all in value."

The king was right in his deductions. In fact, that has been the wise valuation placed on a little child from the days of the birth of the Master himself, who lay in a nest of straw in a manger in Bethlehem of Judea. That child has outweighed all other values since that immortal dawn in Palestine.

And it was he who later, walking along the highway with his disciples, came to a group of mothers out walking with their children. The mothers wanted the Master to bless their children, but the disciples rebuked them. They probably said something like this to them: "Go away. Don't bother the Master. He is busy with many things. He is deep in thought." But Jesus, hearing his disciples, said to them: "Suffer the little children to come unto me, and forbid them not: for of such is the kingdom of God."

He took the children in his arms and blessed them. Then he told those adult disciples that if any man wanted to be worthy of the kingdom he must become as simple, loving, kindly, tolerant, and naive as a little child.

Joaquin Miller, the poet, described the scene in these words:

> Then reaching His hands He said, lowly,
> "Of such is My Kingdom"; and then
> Took the brown little babes in the holy
> White hands of the Savior of men;
>
> Held them close to His heart and carress'd them,
> Put His face down to theirs as in prayer,
> Put their hands to His neck, and so blessed them
> With baby hands hid in His hair.

Yes, the worth of a little child outweighs the material things of the world, and all of us who have or have had children know that as well as the old king in the Talmud knew it.

ờ   ơ

"OUR FAITH TREMENDOUS"

ONE of the friendships over which I am happiest as life moves along its destined way toward the close of my little day is my friendship with Vachel Lindsay, the Illinois poet. He was born on these prairies, and his life was lived out to its end in Springfield, with a few years on other shores and in other towns.

I had the joy of entertaining him in my home; of having him

read his poems in his sing-song, yet haunting fashion to my guests; of having him autograph every single book he ever wrote, with not only prose and poetry in those autographs but those strange hieroglyphics he liked to draw.

The most significant thing he ever said to me was in relation to faith, the faith that he had in himself at times; the faith that sent him tramping the continent selling his own songs like a beggar until he literally forced recognition from this nation for his poems; the faith he had in Lincoln, in Springfield, his own home town; the faith that he had in the citizens of Illinois; the faith he had in our nation in time of war; the faith that he had in the great leaders of our nation; the faith that he had in William Booth, founder of the Salvation Army, a faith he immortalized in "General William Booth enters into Heaven"; the faith he had in American poets, especially midwestern poets like Carl Sandburg, John Neidhardt, Sara Teasdale, and others; the faith he had that his midwestern country could produce great art, poetry, painting, and sculpture. However, the thing which surprised and delighted me was his faith in the religion of the American people. One night he said: "I have tried to express in four lines that faith which is at the core of my existence." Here are the four lines he read to me:

> This is our faith tremendous,
> Our great hope who shall scorn?
> That in the name of Jesus,
> The world shall be reborn.

"What do you mean by that?" I asked him.

"I hesitate to say, with all of my own weaknesses and seeming lack of hope and faith, but since you ask I shall tell you. I mean our faith in the life and personality; the parables and teachings of Jesus, particularly the Sermon on the Mount; the spirit of the Lord's Prayer; the miracles and kindliness of Jesus; the life and loneliness and trial and sufferings and death of the Master. I mean the talk he sent forth to the world of a dream he had of a comrade Kingdom. All of that I tried to sum up in that lit-

131

tle quatrain as my last will and testament of my faith. I hand it to you for whatever use you may want to make of it. This is my faith tremendous."

I go back to that memory often, and I am heartened and strengthened through quoting this document of faith which came to me from Vachel Lindsay:

"This is our faith tremendous,
    Our great hope, who shall scorn?
That in the name of Jesus,
    The world shall be reborn."

ॐ   ॐ

"AFTER THE STORM"

ONE motto which has always helped me through my depression periods, my weeks and months of anxiety, and my troublesome times is the old slogan of the Persian King, "This too shall pass away."

You know the story of how the king sent out a call to all of his wise men to bring him a motto which would serve for good days and bad, for rain and sun, for troublesome days and happy days. Hundreds came in, but this one he chose. "This too shall pass away." He chose that one because it taught him to enjoy any period of happiness to the full, for it too would pass away. While he was miserable that slogan still comforted him, for he said to himself, "This too shall pass away."

In my own family, which is a typical American family, we have used that as a family slogan. When Betty was a child I told her that story, and then later in life when I was troubled and in sore distress she would come gently to me and say: "Don't forget, Dad, what you taught me when I was a child—'This too shall pass away!'" Later, when she had a family of her own and wrote me anxious letters about pressing problems which came to her, I

132

wrote back: "Don't forget our slogan, Betty." So it has been with us as a family; so might it be with all families who read this simple tale.

Here is a bit of poetry which gives a beautiful interpretation of this philosophy of waiting and hoping for a new day and a new dawn of light and sunshine:

> Soft as the voice,
>   As the voice of a zephyr
> Breathing unheard,
>   Hope gently whispers,
> Through the shadows,
>   Her comforting word:
> "Wait 'till the darkness
>   Is over,
> Wait 'till the tempest
>   Is done.
> Hope for the sunshine,
>   Hope for the morrow,
> After the storm."

ঌ   ঽ

LEARNING TO FORGET

EDWIN MARKHAM once told me that he considered his poem "The Hidden Glacier" one of the most significant poems he had ever written. It goes like this:

> There is no time for hate, O wasteful friend:
> Put hate away until the ages end.
> Have you an ancient wound? Forget the wrong. . . .
> Out in my West a forest loud with song
> Towers high and green over a field of snow,
> Over a glacier buried far below.

All of us need to learn the lesson of that simple poem. We

should learn to forget insults—as Abraham Lincoln did. When young McClellan, in arrogant superiority kept him waiting at his tent, Lincoln smiled and said: "I can afford to be insulted if McClellan will but win battles. I bear no hatred or ill-will toward him."

David Lloyd George visited the United States back in the early twenties, and I had the exciting adventure of traveling with him for two days, during which time he told exciting stories of World War I. One of them had to do with an experience he had with Lord Rothschild. Lloyd George, while he was Prime Minister of Great Britain, had trouble with Lord Rothschild over financial matters. They came to hate each other with what seemed to be an implacable hatred. They even attacked each other in Parliament in scathing debate, and the story of their personal enmity came to be one of the scandals of England.

But when the first World War came and Lloyd George was made Chancellor of the Exchequer, the Allies were fighting with their backs to the wall. The situation was desperate. England needed money and needed it desperately. Lloyd George knew that Lord Rothschild could supply that money. One day he said to his secretary, "Send for Rothschild."

His secretary replied, "No, not him!"

"Yes, him! Tell him I want to see him. I need him desperately!"

His secretary still protested, and then Lloyd George had a better thought. "No!" he said. "Come to think of it, I will do better than that. I will go to him. Ask him if he will see me."

He would. So Lloyd George went to his office at once.

Here is the incident as he told it:

When we faced each other I didn't know what he would do, but I reached out my hand and said to him: "We've quarreled in our time, but now we are faced with a problem bigger than either of us. England needs us both! Let's forget the past. Will you?"

"Tell me what I can do to help England and you. I'm ready."

That story points its own moral.

134

ONE ADVENTURE EACH DAY

YEARS ago out in San Francisco, Betty, who was then four years of age, had a great adventure. Her daddy pulled a baby tooth by tying a string to it, tying the string to a door knob, and letting Betty shut the door. Out came the baby tooth; and a sense of triumph came to the young lady.

That evening she wrote this letter to her grandmother:

Dear Grandmother,
    Daddy and Mother pulled my tooth today—mostly Daddy!

Those last two words were emphasized because Betty and her daddy had a little game they had been playing all of her life up to that time and that they have been playing ever since—the game of having at least one adventure each day.

Even that early in life, Betty and her daddy walked across the sand dunes of the Sunset District of San Francisco with the fog from The Golden Gate ocean doorway flying in their faces, imagining that they were pioneer explorers—a sort of Donner Party crossing a hostile continent.

Sometimes they had to create their own adventures if none befell them in the order of events. Often the daily adventure would be that of looking at a sunset on a white cloud sailing through the skies. Because that four-year-old was trained to look at the sunsets, she astonished her grandfather once on a visit back East by crying out one evening. "Oh, Grandfather look at ee bootful sti! Look at ee bootiful sti!"

When Grandfather asked Grandmother what Betty was trying to say, Grandmother replied: "Oh that's some of Will's foolishness. He's always pointing out the sunsets and stars to her."

Well, it may have been some of her daddy's foolishness, but that daddy noticed this summer that Betty's own son, that daddy's grandson, Jacky never saw a cardinal, an oriole, or a red-winged blackbird flash across his vision that he did not come running and saying, "Oh, Da, a bootiful bird!"

It's a good thing to point out the sunsets, the stars, the clouds, the birds, the trees, and other beauties of life to children. It is a good thing to create at least one adventure each day; for the influence extends down generation after generation, training children to get pleasure out of the simple beautiful things which cost nothing and which surround us all. One adventure each day will keep the blues of monotony away.

ʊ   ʊ

"AT ALL THE DOORS"

RECENTLY I read a biography of my friend William Allen White. In it I caught my first clear grasp of the events of the last fifty years of American life. It was a glowing experience to read it, but the most comforting thing I discovered in it was that Mr. White had a nervous breakdown one year and had to go to California for a rest. And the reason I was comforted by that experience in his active life was that so many men—including myself—have had it. While it is a baffling, frightening experience, it is a comfort to know that others have had it and survived.

A few months after I returned, a bit cautious and fearful, to my activities, following a year's enforced rest in California, I received a letter from Bishop George A. Miller, a life-long friend, and he said in that letter:

"Now that you are back in the harness, all of your friends will be telling you to be cautious and not to do it again. I'm doing nothing of the sort. Go to it! We all have to enter the doors that open before us, and Owen Meredith in *Lucile* says something about the fellow who knocked at all the doors of life cautiously, and entered none. Finally, life became to him a noisy affair of the banging and the closing of doors all around the circle of life. He knocked at all the doors of life and entered none. I've seen many men like that in my life all around the earth."

I pass that thought on because it was such a heartening one to

me just when I needed it most. And when I read that biography
of William Allen White, the thing which impressed me most was
the fact that the great events of his life—the glory and the honor,
the power and the influence which he has enjoyed, two of his
great novels, his intimacy with four presidents of the United
States, his national and international reputation—all came after
he had that year of illness and was laid aside and expected
never to do anything.

Evidently when Mr. White came back from his illness he started
right in knocking at all the doors of the White House as confidently as he walked into the door of his Emporia home. He walked
into the door of the life of Woodrow Wilson and wrote a great
book about him. He walked into the tightly shut door of Calvin
Coolidge's life and wrote not one, but two, books about him.

Never could it be said of that smiling, happy, busy man that
"he knocked at all the doors of life and entered none."

ꙮ ꙮ

THE SHIP OF HOPE

WHEN I was an egotistical young man I was once talking with
Bishop Edwin Holt Hughes. We were talking about death, and
I said rather boastfully: "I never write or preach about death!"

That wise bishop turned to me with a gentle rebuke and said:
"Then, Will, you leave out of your preaching the one universal
fact and experience of life, don't you?"

I have never since that rebuke left out of my thoughts, my writing, or my public speaking, the universal experience of death.
This leads me into the most helpful and interesting parable on
death I have ever found, the author of which is one of those unknown geniuses of the long ago. It reads:

I am standing upon the seashore. A ship at my side spreads her white
sails to the morning breeze and starts for the blue ocean.

137

She is an object of beauty and strength, and I stand and watch her until at length she is only a ribbon of white cloud just where the sea and sky come to mingle with each other. Then someone at my side says: "There! She's gone!"

Gone where? Gone from my sight—that is all. She is just as large in mast and hull and spar as she was when she left my side, and just as able to bear her load of living freight—to the place of destination.

Her diminished size is in me, not in her, and just at the very moment some one at my side says: "There! She's gone!"—there are other voices ready to send up the glad shout: "There! She's come!" And that my friends, is dying!"

So runs the parable on death and immortality, and such is the faith of Christian peoples everywhere. Edwin Markham puts it this way:

> No soul can be forever banned,
> Eternally bereft:
> Whoever falls from God's right hand
> Is caught into His left.

ᴐ ᴄ

MIRACLE MAGNETS

SEVERAL years ago I lived in San Francisco near the sand dunes of the Golden Gate, in what they call the Sunset District. I used to take my daughter Betty on walks through the dunes, and we would always take a small magnet with us and run it through the sand, which is full of small particles of iron.

With each sweep of the small magnet through the sand we could gather up a thimbleful of iron particles. One day I tried to teach Betty a lesson which would hold for life by telling her that the grateful, kind, appreciative person was like that magnet; that such a person would inevitably attract gratitude, kindness, and appreciation from other people. Then I asked her to run her hand through the sand to see if it would draw iron particles. It did not. Then I tried to tell her that was exactly like indifferent, unloving, and unappreciative people; that they could not and would not attract such virtues to themselves; that people had to have what I have always liked to call "the attitude of gratitude" in themselves in order to attract such things from others.

I did not use such adult terms in talking with Betty when she was only four years of age, but used words which she could understand at that time. My system of education worked wonders, for she is now, in her womanhood, about the most appreciative person I know, and she attracts people to her as a magnet attracts iron particles.

I thought that I was original in the use of that figure of a magnet, but twenty years later I was reading some of Henry Ward Beecher's sermons and found the same idea there. Dr. Beecher lived as long ago as 1813-1887, and when I read his sermons I discovered that I had been scooped in that particular figure of speech that far back.

What he actually said was this: "If one should give me a dish of sand, and tell me that there were particles of iron in it, I might look for them with my eyes and search for them with my clumsy fingers and never detect them; but let me take a magnet and sweep it through that dish of sand, and that magnet would draw those tiny particles of iron to it through the power of its attraction! The unthankful heart, like my finger in the sand, discovers no mercies; but let the thankful heart sweep through the day, and, as the magnet finds the iron, so it will find in every hour some heavenly blessings, only the iron in God's hand is gold!"

Yes, the attitude of gratitude is a magnet which draws beauty, love, friendship, appreciation, and loyalty from others. It was so back in 1915, when Betty and I walked the sand dunes of San Francisco. It was so back in the early part of the last century, when Henry Ward Beecher lived. It will be so through all the centuries to come.

❧   ❦

ACKNOWLEDGMENTS

ACKNOWLEDGMENT is due the following authors, publishers, and holders of copyrights for their gracious permission to reproduce in this volume the selections noted:

Bess Streeter Aldrich and D. Appleton-Century Company for selection from *Song of Years.*

Brandt & Brandt for lines from "The Concert" by Edna St. Vincent Millay.

Harper & Brothers for selections from *Silver in the Sun* by Grace Noll Crowell.

Houghton Mifflin Company for lines from "After Sunset" by Grace Hazard Conkling.

The Macmillan Company for lines from "Foreign Missions in Battle Array" from *Collected Poems* by Vachel Lindsay.

Virgil Markham for selections from poems by his father, Edwin Markham

Juanita J. Miller for lines from "Byron" and "Beyond Jordan" by her father, Joaquin Miller.

Angela Morgan for lines from "Stand Forth."

INDEX OF TITLES

144

INDEX OF PERSONS

147

INDEX OF TOPICS

151

"The robber is robbed by his riches," Edwin Markham, 100

"This is our faith tremendous," Vachel Lindsay, 131

"When you've got a thing to say," Joel Chandler Harris, 56

"Yet as I lived them, strange I did not know," Grace Noll Crowell, 79

Prayer, 23, 41, 68

Radiating, 28, 50, 97, 114, 138
Radium, 50
Religion, 39, 40, 89, 109, 130
Remembering, 27, 84, 116, 118, 119
Restitution, 17
Revenge, 99, 133
Reverence, 68, 78, 82, 94, 127

Sacrifice, 57
Scientists, 47, 50, 62
Seeds, 81
Sensitiveness, 100
Service
  doctor's, 57
  food administration (Hoover), 24
  rewards for, 72
  spirit and acts of, 48, 64, 65, 68
Sharing, 12, 17, 18, 24, 32, 45, 64, 65, 88, 96
Simplicity, 14, 15, 92
Sin, 76, 99, 133
Singing, 61, 83, 109, 118
Social movements, 42
Sorrow, 81
Soul, 78

Splendor, 72
Stability, 11, 71, 121
Stars, 123
Storms, 90, 106
Strength
  President Roosevelt, 107
  "Three Words of," 37
Struggle, 31, 85, 107, 115
Suffering, 81, 105

Testimony, 13, 87
Time, 34, 82, 119, 133
Triumph, 107
Truth, 123

Values, 129
Victory, 28
Vision, 21, 27, 54, 62, 90, 107, 110, 115, 135

War, 83, 123, 134
Wealth, 46, 98
Wind, 41, 90, 106
Wings, 44
Woods, 30
Work, 114
Worry, 37, 105

Youth
  Henry Luce, editor, 14
  Herbert Hoover, when, 17, 24
  inspiration to, 28
  son, 15

Zephyr, 133